How to Write Training Materials

How to Write Training Materials

Linda Stoneall

San Diego • Toronto • Amsterdam • Sydney

ISBN: 0-88390-291-5

Library of Congress Catalog Number: 91-11344

Printed in the United States of America

Library of Congress Cataloging-in-Publication Data

Stoneall, Linda.
    How to write training materials / Linda Stoneall.
        p.   cm.
    Includes bibliographical references and index.
    ISBN 0-88390-291-5 (alk. paper)
    1. Training manuals. 2. Employees—Training of. I. Title.

HF5549.5.T7272 1991   91-11344
658.3'12404—dc20   CIP

Pfeiffer & Company
8517 Production Avenue
San Diego, California 92121
Telephone (619) 578-5900
FAX (619) 578-2042

TABLE OF CONTENTS

1

INTRODUCTION

A district manager—let's call him George—received an assignment to provide the managers in his district with management training. He and other executives had received complaints and even threats of lawsuits from employees because managers were firing employees at whim. George was very concerned and highly motivated to change his managers, and he knew that he could relate well to them. His goal was to have his managers follow a discipline policy, and he had a one-page outline of topics to cover that included stating expectations, giving warnings, and writing documentation—actions which he himself had never taken. George also had handouts and an overhead transparency of the policy that the legal department had written.

The meeting was scheduled to last two hours, but George, not a talkative man, covered the points in a few minutes. The managers could not read the small print from the overhead projector, and they could not understand the legal jargon on the handout. The managers did not want to make themselves look bad, so they did not ask questions. Nothing changed.

What could have helped George? Answer: a better script.

Written instructions are essential for successful training, but written materials alone are not sufficient. The instructions must be sufficiently detailed for trainers with various backgrounds to use them with the same results. The materials should also be well written: they must maximize communication between trainer and trainee and should be interesting—even fun—to use. The purpose of this book is to help training designers to write thoroughly and to write well.

Writing can be trainers' most important activity, both because the written word can reach a wider audience and because written material lasts longer than presentations. The writing of training materials is the start of a chain that influences many people. The process of writing can generate creative excitement, with new ideas growing as fast as the writer can set them down. It can also seem like hard work, especially when no ideas come at all. This book is designed for both the creative thrill and the frustration of writer's block.

Training designers are the playwrights of adult education. They amass their creativity, their ideas, and their craft to create the materials that trainers need in order to perform well. Like playwrights, designers may need to rewrite the script several times, but it is exciting to see one's work "performed" as the writer had envisioned it. It is gratifying to see employees who like their jobs better and who work more efficiently as a result of training. Executives, too, often have praise for the training designer whose efforts contribute to reductions in employee turnover, errors, and complaints.

The playscript analogy illustrates the level of detail that works best. Training writers should write out what the presenters say, what questions they ask, and how they should organize groups and activities. The presenters eventually will distill the script or leader's guide into a manageable outline, incorporating their own cues and lines. Of course, trainers use their own words. The written design is simply a guide for trainers to what types of things they should say. For example, the play *The Wiz* is the same story as the film *The Wizard of Oz,* which illustrates that a script allows for creative interpretation.

Many purchased or in-house training programs are just outlines or lists of objectives. However, a shortened design may not provide the trainer with enough information. The example of George, who had only one page of notes, is evidence of this. Only the highly talented, highly knowledgeable expert can succeed with such a brief outline. Using a detailed training guide increases the chances of success with a greater variety of trainers.

Although the leader's guide should be detailed, it need not be an annotated book. To use the example of the play, a finished play does not include all of the research, the background, and the interviews that went into the three acts. The writer needs to give the presenter enough information to make the two-hour or five-day presentation without overwhelming the presenter. It may be helpful to include some background information to help the presenter to answer questions. If the presenter is inexperienced, he or she can obtain background information through train-the-trainer courses, through reference reading, or through a summary of the researcher's findings.

Writing the design in the form of a script has many benefits. Not only does a script enable the person without in-depth subject matter to conduct training, it also promotes trainers' consistency and accountability. In other words, measurements of the training are valid and reliable, regardless of who does the training. In addition, a clearly written design becomes a legal document that can help an organization's defense if needed in court.

CONSISTENCY

Trainers will of course use their own words, gestures, and personal examples, but the detailed training guide will help to keep them on track. Trainers are expected not only to meet the same objectives each time they teach a particular course but to meet those objectives in the same way—a "Howard Johnson's" approach to training. Training often sets standards and expectations for jobs. In addition, each employee hired to fill a particular position should receive the same type of training in the interest of fairness. Furthermore, one of the purposes of training is to promote safety and efficiency. If the training is about how to use a machine, for example, varying the training could result in misuse of the machine or even damage to the machine or its users. Consistency in training also contributes to equality in policies, especially across branches of a large organization.

Clear and well-written handouts and overhead slides also contribute to learning and retention. If, in the previous example, George had had more readable overhead slides and other visual aids, the managers might have become more interested in the topic. If they had received handouts that encouraged them to take notes and that made note taking easier, they would have been more likely to remember what they learned and to use that information back on the job.

ACCOUNTABILITY

Training materials also help to make the presenters accountable. A script of what the trainer should do and say clearly states expectations and performance standards. The written design itself can serve as a checklist for the presenter's supervisor to ensure that the presenter covers all points, discussions, and activities. For example, if a supervisor realizes that the trainer has left out an important step, such as directing the trainees to try out a particular skill, he or she may feel the need to coach the trainer.

The leader's guide, though detailed, still leaves room to customize the program. For example, the facilitator can downplay certain points that the whole group already understands or uses. The writer can also build in options for the facilitator: an optional video or a choice of activities, for example. The writer could also leave holes in the program that the trainer can fill with examples from his or her personal experiences.

LEGAL ASPECTS

A written design has legal advantages because it documents what took place in the training session. A written design shows that trainers exposed employees to certain information about their jobs. As such, courts can subpoena training plans and other training materials as evidence.

Training guides back the company's actions and intents. For example, when a male employee claimed wrongful termination and sued his organization, the company stated that he had been terminated on the grounds of sexual harassment. The employee testified that he did not know that he was doing wrong. However, a training guide for a course on sexual harassment proved that the organization informed its employees of the wrongfulness of telling offensive jokes and the consequences of continuing such behavior.

The training design may state job expectations and may also instruct employees in how to fulfill these expectations. However, lawyers caution that a lesson plan should not imply that a job description or list of tasks are definitive. If it does, the organization may have problems; employees can find something that they were not told and can use that against their employers. Organizations also benefit if the trainer takes attendance and—even better—conducts some type of inventory at the end of the training to measure the extent to which each employee understood what was taught.

SUMMARY OF BOOK

New designers may want to supplement the information in this book with books on adult-learning theory. After becoming familiar with training principles, they may wish to reread this book, then go back to individual chapters while working on each part of the training design. One aim of this book is to show the reader how to translate ideas into simple, concise prose. More experienced readers may wish to use individual chapters to get writing ideas for particular tasks. Each chapter begins with a case study that raises the issues addressed in that chapter. These cases are fictionalized and are not intended to depict the experiences of any person or organization.

Chapter 2, "Research Writing," explains how research writing can be helpful in the development of training materials. The kinds of notes designers record when they observe and participate in jobs, when they read on the subject, and when they interview experts make it easier to create lesson plans and learning activities. Interview and survey questions must be skillfully worded to elicit the most useful and truthful responses. Ways to code or organize the results of this research also will be discussed.

Chapter 3, "Writing a Training Map," discusses how to get started. The designer first selects and develops concepts; the plan and flow of the training program emerge from these concepts. Writers can use outlines, flow charts, and symbols to draw their "maps." As we will see, how the writer sets down his or her objectives is critical to this step.

Chapter 4, "Writing the Detailed Design," addresses the subject of telling the trainer what to say. In short, trainers should tell their audience what they are going to say, tell them, and then tell them what they just said. Designers have the choice of writing a word-for-word speech or of simply writing phrases that will guide a trainer. Chapter 4 also discusses writing introductions, instructions for skills and concepts, and examples to illustrate the point. Readers will also learn how to record transitions among the parts and how to summarize.

Chapter 5, "Writing Learning Activities," tells the trainer how to get audiences more active and involved. Included are suggestions such as prepared discussion questions and answers to those questions. Readers will also learn how to write instructions for setting up role plays, case studies, simulations, games, and other learning activities, which many writers find enjoyable.

Chapter 6, "Writing Handouts and Training Manuals," discusses effective writing for trainees. Writers should use a different language for trainees than for trainers. They need to speak in the trainees' words and to write on the trainees' reading level. This chapter includes suggestions such as: words, short phrases, or questions that can help trainees to take notes. Sometimes text is helpful; sometimes outlines are more effective. The use of work sheets can direct students in learning activities during the training session as well as on the job.

Chapter 7, "Writing Videoscripts," tells readers how to write scripts that reinforce learning. Readers will learn how to write dialogue, narrative, and drama. Designers who are familiar with these skills can write videoscripts for use outside the classroom or to illustrate the skills in action. Videoscripts enable students to practice by responding to a scene or interaction. Trainees can also analyze negative examples for further learning. Designers often find themselves with the task of writing the messages or questions that appear on the screen. With the use of computer-assisted instruction or interactive video, writers can add responses to learners' answers.

Chapter 8, "Writing Evaluations and Measurements," discusses ways of writing tests and evaluations. The chapter presents the pros and cons of open-ended, multiple-choice, matching, and true-false questions. Readers will also learn ways to write checklists and other evaluations designed to measure trainers' performance.

Chapter 9, "Supervising Writers of Training Materials," suggests efficient methods of managing others' writing. It describes what to look for in others' writing, how to give feedback, and how to train others to write training materials.

Good luck with this book and happy writing!

2

RESEARCH WRITING

Kate, the training director, asked Amy, a novice training designer, to research a communication program for supervisors in their organization. Amy telephoned the supervisors' managers and asked, "How do your supervisors communicate?"

One answered, "Okay, I guess."

The next manager asked, "What do you mean by 'communicate'?" Amy had no answer.

Because she did not seem to be getting any information from the managers, Amy decided to survey the supervisors instead. She had read a few books and articles on communication and her notes stressed the following topics:

- listening
- questioning
- giving instructions
- empathizing
- summarizing

From her reading, she constructed the questionnaire in Figure 2-1.

The supervisors who returned the survey answered every question with a four or a five on the continuum, which indicated a high level of satisfaction. Kate asked Amy for a report of the survey results. Amy's brief report (see

To: Supervisors
From: Amy Ross
Please answer the following questions:

How well do you *listen?*

Very well					Not at all
5	4	3	2	1	0

How well do you *question?*

Very well					Not at all
5	4	3	2	1	0

How well do you *give instructions?*

Very well					Not at all
5	4	3	2	1	0

How well do you *empathize?*

Very well					Not at all
5	4	3	2	1	0

How well do you *summarize?*

Very well					Not at all
5	4	3	2	1	0

What could you do to improve communication in your department?

Figure 2-1. Amy's Questionnaire

Figure 2-2) indicated that (1) most people thought they communicated well, (2) some supervisors saw a need for better employees, and (3) many supervisors saw no problems with communication.

After Kate read the report she asked Amy, "How will you design the program?" Unfortunately, Amy's survey had not given her any ideas because her research had not helped her to understand the problem or even to decide whether a problem existed; she had not uncovered a need. Kate, who had given the assignment to Amy, said that she had heard complaints, and that the executives wanted communication training to be conducted. However, Kate had told Amy that the executives could not take the time to answer any research questions, and Amy's survey had not uncovered any communication problems. Let's look at what Amy could have done.

Amy made mistakes that better writing could have prevented. She failed to word her telephone questions in a way that would prompt the managers to give her valuable information. She could have created clear, specific questions for the supervisors' survey, administered them orally, and taken detailed notes on the answers so that she could write a helpful, accurate summary of the results.

Number of supervisors responding to survey: 11

Number of supervisors scoring high on all questions: 11

Typical comments: "Don't have a problem," "Some employees don't listen or don't care or both," "I give clear instructions, yet employees keep doing things the same old way."

Figure 2-2. Report on Amy's Communication Survey

WAYS AND MEANS OF RESEARCH

Before beginning any research, writers need to ask themselves one question: Why am I doing research in the first place? Usually, writers conduct research in order to uncover information that they need to help them write training programs. Writers can learn from what other organizations do and from what other people have written or said. They also may learn more about the organization's need for the program. In other words, the process of research aids needs assessment and also informs the designer about the subject matter.

People decide that there is a need for training programs by comparing the real with the ideal, what is to how it should be. The purpose of research is to discover both the real and the ideal by examining a job, what the people who hold that job say and think about it, and what alternatives exist. The designer may choose to examine a few situations in depth or to stay with the surface issues in order to examine a broader range of cases. Ideally, the training designer should begin with in-depth study, which will indicate which questions to ask, and then the designer should question many people.

This chapter follows the ideal pattern. It begins with in-depth observations, reading, and note taking. Next, the chapter discusses interviewing and the corresponding questions and notes. Finally, this chapter discusses surveys and the writing of questionnaires, including a discussion of how to write codes and reports on the findings of the research.

Taking Notes

Good writing in note taking helps to accomplish the following:

- Helps you to remember;

- Facilitates good communication between the note taker and others who may help to design the program; and
- Preserves materials more accurately for later use in training programs.

The only researchers who do not need to take notes are those with perfect memories and no other projects; in other words, all researchers should take notes! If, in the previous example, Amy had worked with a team or if someone had had to take over her project, detailed notes would have speeded communication and prevented others from doing tasks twice.
Researchers can take notes on any or all of the following:

- Things they read: books, articles, records, and other writings;
- Things they watch: videotapes, external presentations, and people at work; and
- Things they hear: audiotapes, speeches, and lectures.

The observation of people at work is in a slightly different category from the other forms of collecting data. During observation the researcher is collecting first-hand (primary) data. In contrast, the other methods of research involve the unearthing of information that someone else has already collected and filtered (secondary data). Both secondary and primary data can be useful in conducting research.

Secondary Data

The collection of secondary data serves two main functions. First, it can serve as a guide to primary research, and writers can use secondary information directly in the training design. Secondary data provides the researcher with a lot of background information at little effort. A researcher can learn a great deal about both broad and specific topics by reading books or by going through a program. Books and other learning programs can provide researchers with information that they would not have been able to find on their own, with a minimum of effort and with another person's expertise. Researchers can then use their learnings to help them understand others in their organizations. For example, some knowledge of computers will help a training designer to understand the special needs and problems of computer users and will enable them to design more useful and current training sessions. Secondary data can become an integral part of the training design itself; researchers can borrow anything from a whole program to the learning activity down to a quote or statistic to convince an audience.

Different methods of note taking work for different types of research, depending on how thoroughly the researcher wants to record the data. Outlines, lists, and diagrams work well for taking notes on background information, how something works, or relevant concepts. It is not necessary to master roman numerals or flow-chart symbols in order to make outlines or diagrams; the important thing is to be able to remember and to communicate the information. Record the main points only; it is not necessary to write in complete sentences.

Figure 2-3 gives an example of notes on how to ride a bicycle.

---

1. Hold bicycle upright.

2. Straddle bar.

3. Sit on seat.

4. Push off with one leg.

5. Pedal the bicycle smoothly and rhythmically.

Figure 2-3. Notes on How to Ride a Bicycle

Amy's notes were lists of concepts. She needed more detail on how the concepts worked: What steps does a person take to complete the skills? What is the order of those steps? Use whole sentences when recording quotes and definitions. It is especially important to record quotes (written and spoken) word for word in order to be able to reprint them verbatim. With notes of lists or definitions, it is helpful to record some of the author's examples, because examples remind the note taker of the meaning and use of the concept. Authors and speakers will sometimes refer to other sources; it is important to take down all information necessary to accurately reference—and perhaps to obtain permission for—cited material. Write the name of the publisher, the title, the author's name, and the publication date. Record any thoughts and questions that the reading or listening inspires. These thoughts and questions will be the start of the primary research.

Below is an example of how a reseacher might take notes as the speaker reads from Hayakawa, (1954):

S.I. Hayakawa, 1954, p. 105. "Listening means trying to see the problem the way the speaker sees it....Listening requires entering actively and imaginatively into the other person's situation and trying to understand a frame of reference different than your own." Example: "Imagine being on a new job... listening instead of advising, directing..."

Many of the rules for researching scholarly articles do not apply to the note-taking process. For example, source listings do not have to follow the strict format of the American Psychological Association, nor do the notes themselves need to be in any certain format. Source listings and notes need only to be legible and clear.

Taking notes on index cards can be advantageous because the cards are portable; they can be sorted and arranged in many different ways. On the other hand, taking notes on notebook or legal-sized paper is often easier and has the advantage of being less easily lost or misplaced than note cards. Some people prefer to type notes to make them more legible.

Primary Data

Observing and interviewing provides primary data. Observing is useful when employees may not be aware of what they do or why, or when employees may not be able to put their jobs into words. An observer also can see the interaction between several people working together on a project and may even recognize processes and interactions of which the employees themselves are not aware. Of course, if the training designer once held the job for which he or she will be conducting training, first-hand observation may be unnecessary.

As a case in point, first-hand observation would have given Amy much more information about how supervisors actually communicate. She then would have known what questions to ask, had a better idea about the supervisors' needs, and gleaned many examples to use in her training design.

The first step when observing is usually to conduct a job analysis by recording all the tasks that make up a job. Here, the best writing technique is to use verbs: What happens first? Then what? Do not omit anything at first, even if it seems obvious. For example: He

- walks to door
- inserts key
- unlocks the door
- pulls open the handle

Note taking usually occurs at an early stage of observation when the designer is trying to decide what to cover. Until a decision is made, it is wise to take notes on everything. Trying to record everything forces people to be more objective. Plus, these notes will provide fodder for video-tapes, case studies, and examples. At a later stage of note taking, when designers have pinpointed specific topics, they will limit note taking to that topic. For example, a trainer may be developing a program to train people to operate a machine. First, the trainer will take notes about all aspects of the machine; later, the trainer will focus on how to start and stop the machine or any other important features or processes that the trainees should learn.

Some purposes of observation are to discover all of the components that constitute a particular job or to look for mistakes that people make or things that they omit or overdo. Notes taken during observation should record people's actions and the context of those actions. Conversations and statements should be recorded word for word; note, also, people's body language while they are speaking. Observations about body language are especially important in preparation for communication and management programs. Figure 2-4 shows a sample recording form.

Place: Payroll office
Date: October 15, 1990
Time: 9:00 a.m.

Supervisor	**Employee**	**Others Present**
What are you doing over there?		All Payroll employees
	Just getting a drink.	
Get back to work. I need that printout by 9:15.		

Figure 2-4. Sample Recording Form

Training designers also should note their feelings and actions—of difficulty, of frustration, of mistakes, and so on—if they are participating in the job. Checklists can be helpful in recording specific 'actions and body language. Figure 2-5 illustrates a checklist.

After recording observations, the training designer must analyze and code the notes. This need not be elaborate; researchers can write codes in the margins of the notes. Keep in mind that the object is to obtain information on a particular job and what skills and knowledge employees need to obtain in order to do their jobs better.

Designers can count frequencies as part of the analysis. For example, how often do employees defend their own positions with a client instead of listening to the client? When this occurs, designers can write "defensive" in the margins of their notes. At the end, they can total the "defensives" and compare them as percentages to the total number of interactions. These types of statistics can be valuable measures of training success when compared with post-training observations.

It may also be helpful to analyze the kinds of words and statements that people used. For example, a supervisor may use a lot of commands rather than "I" statements or expla-

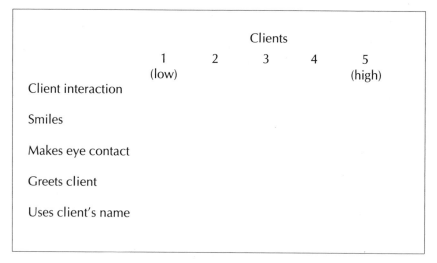

Figure 2-5. Sample Checklist

nations. The commands could be underlined and noted in the margins. It is also important to note when the mistake or omission occurs. Consider the time of day, the content of disagreements, and the characteristics of the people involved. This may indicate whether the problem is a training problem or whether to target training to a select group.

INTERVIEW QUESTIONS

While a training designer is observing people at work he or she may participate in the work in order to understand the particular mechanics and problems of the job. In that case, the notes will consist mainly of observations and impressions of the job. Sometimes the training designer will have held the job that he or she is observing. However, it is not safe to assume that all people experience a job in the same way. Therefore, the training designer will need to interview people to discover how they perceive and feel about their jobs, what motivates them, and why they believe that the organization's "standard operating procedures" exist.

Interviews may be conducted in person or over the phone. Tape recording interviews should be done only with the interviewee's permission. Over-the-phone interviews can save travel time and may avoid interruptions. Another method of interviewing is the focus group, in which the interviewer talks to several people at once.

All interviews require prework (prepared questions) and follow-up (analysis of notes). Because some people can easily think of questions as they talk with others, the need to prepare interview questions may not immediately be evident. However, in order to compare people's responses, one must be consistent by asking everyone the same questions, by wording the questions identically, and by asking each person *all* of the questions. Having a list of questions will take the guesswork out of the interview process. Written questions also help to keep the interviewer on track. Some employees may have fascinating stories to tell, which can distract the interviewer from his or her true purpose: to find out about that person's job needs. Written questions can also help to maximize the interview time. If the interviewees receive the questions ahead of time, they can be thinking about the topics and about what they want to tell the interviewer. Well-written questions are, of course, essential. Finally, preparing interview questions in advance allows the interviewer to delegate some of the work.

Writing the Interview Questions

In order to compile a list of questions, the interviewer must first decide on the topics. Next, the interviewer should arrange the questions in a logical order. Start with impersonal, nonthreatening questions such as:

- What did you do today on the job?
- What do you like best about your job?

Save any personal, hard-to-answer questions (such as questions about feelings, sensitive issues, and dislikes) for the latter part of the interview, by which time the interviewer will have had a chance to develop some rapport with the interviewee. This allows interviewees to become more comfortable, thus increasing the chances that they will open up and give more revealing responses. Other possible arrangements might be by the order in which they are performed (e.g., the steps of a process), or by the magnitude of the problem (beginning with smaller problems and working up to larger ones).

Journalists ask four "W" questions *(who, what, when, where)* plus one "H" question *(how)*. Questions that begin with one of these words ask for more information than imple yes-or-no questions; they also encourage people to open up about themselves. If most of the questions call for yes-or-no answers, consider conducting a survey rather than taking the time to interview. On the other hand, questions that are too broad—such as Amy's "How do your supervisors communicate?"—are difficult to answer because people do not know where to begin. If the topic is broad, the questions need to be broken down into smaller, more specific components of the main topic. A topic that does not seem to be divisible may actually be a signal to the interviewer to conduct more research and observation in order to understand the subject matter better.

Some observers and interviewers ask about events as they occur: "What did that mean? How do you feel about that?" People will not have prerehearsed their answers and may therefore respond more truthfully.

"Why" questions often come later in the interview, often immediately following one of the other "W" questions. For example, "What's the first thing you do with a new employee? Why do you do that?" At this point in the interview, the list of questions should include not only "why" prompts but reminders to *probe*. Good interviewers do not write down people's first responses to questions and stop; they ask questions from different angles, ask about additional points mentioned in the initial responses, and so on. An example of a good probe is "What's an example of that?" Answers to this question will help the interviewer to analyze the conditions of various situations.

To compose interview questions, try to use the language of the interviewees. For example, an interview with a doctor should include the medical terms with which he or she is familiar. Be sure that the interviewees understand the words of the interview questions. For example, do not say, "How do you mirror the client?" if the interviewee will not understand what "mirroring" is.

During the Interview

You should now be ready to interview. Write down what the interviewees say, word for word. This method is faster than recording the conversation on tape and then having to transcribe it. Note taking also allows the interviewer to record body language that would be lost if the interview were taped. Some interviewers find a combination of notetaking and tape recording to be most satisfactory. They can take notes on important statements and body language, supplementing them with more lengthy, accurate quotes from the audiotape later.

WRITING THE QUESTIONNAIRE

If all the interview questions require only short answers, choices between alternatives, or a limited list of possibilities, it may be more efficient to survey. Questionnaires can also be helpful when polling a large sample or simply as a method of distributing information. Just as interviewers use checklists to observe, employees can check off information about their tasks from a prepared list. Although questionnaires are not as thorough as interviews or observation, they enable interviewers to poll a larger sample and to get a better idea of the organizational situation across the board. However, interviewing is still the method of choice for finding specific examples or for discovering new issues.

Surveys excel when the object is to learn people's opinions because of the anonymity. Surveys can also ask about topics that people will not discuss with others (think of the Hite sex surveys). On the organizational level, surveys can be used to learn about employee theft or other taboo topics.

Survey-question writing requires even more care and precision than interview-question writing because the surveyor usually will not be able to talk with people about their responses. The people filling out the survey should have no doubt about what the questions are; otherwise, the answers will be inconsistent and therefore inconclusive. Survey instructions must be as well written as the questions themselves, especially because the instructions often state the reason for the survey. A clever surveyor will motivate people by telling them what is in it for them. Realize that "It's your duty to the company" motivates precious few. Surveys can offer money as an incentive, but persuasion ("Your answers can make a difference in your working conditions") can be the most convincing. Figure 2-6 provides a sample survey introduction.

The XYZ Company would like to create a management-trainee program that will specify all requirements. This will make a promotion for you easier and quicker. To create the program, we would like to know your needs and wants; we also need to know what aspects of the current program could be improved. Please be candid. Any information that you provide will remain anonymous and confidential.

Figure 2-6. Sample Survey Introduction

What kinds of survey questions should a researcher write?

(a) Open-ended questions

(b) Short-answer questions

(c) Multiple-choice questions

Of the above choices, "multiple-choice questions" is the correct answer, because these work best for surveys. Researchers also employ scales, checklists, and yes-no questions. All of these are easier to answer and easier to code than open-ended or short-answer questions. Responses to short-answer and open-ended questions are often vague and, therefore, more subject to interpretation. Open-ended questions could elicit more detailed information, but they tend to produce maximal results only with articulate, educated people and are therefore not the right choice for every survey situation. Of course, poorly written questions can diminish the usefulness of any survey. It is a good idea to get some demographic information (e.g., sex, age, length of time on the job, position) about the people being surveyed; this will help to indicate whether needs are pervasive or whether they are confined to certain groups.

WRITING SURVEY QUESTIONS

It is important to make it as easy as possible for a person to fill out the survey. If the survey is difficult to understand, people will be far less likely to complete it. Make each question short and simple. Use easy-to-understand words in simple sentences. Do not include absolute words (always, never, ever) in the question, because conditions are rarely absolute. Keep in mind that the fewer the number of questions, the higher the response rate.

Rather than asking people taking the survey to write, give them lines or boxes to check. The choices should also make the desired type of answer clear—there will always be a person who writes "often" if the question merely states "Sex?" A better question would be:

Sex: M___   F___

One can ask about age in several ways. The question "Age?" or "How old are you?" may prompt questions from people who have birthdays that week and do not know how to answer. A more accurate method would be to ask, "On what date were you born?" Some surveys do not require that much accuracy; in that case, age options could be grouped for easier coding. For example:

Age:
0-19___   20-29___   30-39___
40-49___   50 +___

This method also works when asking a person's length of service in a job. One can ask people to select from ranges or to state their date of hire. The next categories of questions should be about tasks or attitudes. These questions can be arranged in several ways. Multiple-choice questions work best if the choices are limited—to no more than six or seven choices. Be sure to phrase each option in such a way that the survey taker must choose only one. If everyone checks off every choice, no useful data has been collected. It is also best to ask about specifics because information will tend to be more accurate. For example:

1. *How often do you take a break?*

   Every two hours ___

   Every four hours ___

   Whenever I feel like it ___

2. *How long did your last break last?*

   Ten minutes ___

   Fifteen minutes ___

   Twenty minutes ___

   Longer than twenty minutes___

An alternative to multiple-choice questions is the method called *ranking.* Ranking asks people to list the order in which they prefer a list of items or, perhaps, to prioritize the reasons that they do something. It is imperative that respondents understand the questions and the directions. Not only must their vocabulary be used, but the choices must be distinctive with no overlap. The surveyor can test the survey by asking people who meet similar criteria as those being surveyed to take the survey and to make suggestions.

Ranking questions should list the choices randomly, not by any personal preferences that could bias the responses. For example:

Training designers have four major tasks. Rank them in order of difficulty to you, "1" being the most difficult and "4" being the least difficult.

Writing tests ___   Writing videoscripts___

Writing handouts___   Writing objectives___

Scaled questions differ from ranking questions. Scaled questions ask respondents to rate the degree of something, for example, their agreement or disagreement with a statement. Scaled questions also can ask respondents to rate such factors as importance, frequency, and difficulty. The usual range is from one to five, but scales from one to seven or ten also exist.   Vary the order of the scales in order to make readers pay more attention. This may prevent the tendency to check the same column every time. Figure 2-7 provides a sample.

Another survey technique is to create a checklist or table with columns for each possible response. An example is given in Figure 2-8.

Completed surveys are easy to tally: simply count the frequency of each response, a process similar to that of observational coding. Computers can facilitate the scoring of statistical tests.

REPORTING THE FINDINGS

Notes, interview questions, and surveys generate a great deal of data. Before analyzing the data for its benefits to training, you may want to communicate the results.

Just as Kate wanted a summary of Amy's survey, your supervisor may want one also. One way to do this is to list

How difficult is it for you to close up at night?

very difficult   very easy

1   2   3   4   5

How much time do you spend closing up at night?

little time   much time

5   4   3   2   1

How important is closing up at night in relation to your other tasks?

very important   not important

1   2   3   4   5

Figure 2-7. Sample Variety of Survey Scales

Skill	I do this WELL	I am about AVERAGE	I could use IMPROVEMENT
Defining problems			
Listing solutions			
Developing criteria for decision making			
Making action plans			

Figure 2-8. Sample Table for Survey

the questions along with the answers, but the summary will be more informative if the answers have frequency counts and are ranked in order. An example is given in Figure 2-9.

Question 1. Why did you leave your job?

Not enough responsibility 10

Mistreatment by supervisor 8

Inability to do the job   7

Figure 2-9. Sample Summary of Survey

Supervisors sometimes have time only to read a page or less of the report. If this is the case, the summary can simply include the questions and the range of answers. Accompany the data with a one-page report, either in short paragraphs or in a list. Tell what kinds of questions were included and why. Report on participation rates and ranges of answers. Be sure to answer the following:

- How many people answered?

- What were the two extremes in their answers?

- What were the average or more frequent training needs?

- How will you use this information? What solution(s) do you suggest?

Figure 2-10 provides a sample summary of survey findings.

Report on Needs Assessment, ABC Branch

- 25 out of 30 employees responded.

- with the ABC Branch for 1 to 10 years, an average of 3 years.

- supervised 1 to 7 years, average of 2.

- 10 problems reported. Eight of the ten respondents began supervising within the past year.

- The number-one problem: disciplining employees (12 responses).

- The number-two problem: getting people to meet minimum performance (10 responses).

Recommendation: training workshop on communicating standards and expectations; follow-up on expectations and standards with regard to motivation and discipline.

Figure 2-10. Sample Summary of Survey Findings

CHAPTER SUMMARY

The purpose of conducting research before writing training materials is to learn more about concepts and skills and to determine training needs. Clear, concise writing and note-taking skills are essential components of good research. Good notes will jog the memory, communicate to others, and preserve data for use in training materials. Careful observation is another method of gathering information. Well-written questions are essential to the good interview. Survey questions must be easy to understand; otherwise, responses may not be valid.

The research and accompanying summary is merely preparation for the real task: the design and development of a training program. Here, too, good writing is essential. A "map" or outline with identified objectives can make the writing of the actual lesson plan much easier.

REFERENCES

Hayakawa, S.I. (1954). How to attend a conference. In S.I. Hayakawa (Ed.), *Etc.—our language — our world: Selections; a review of general semantics* (pp. 103-110). New York: Harper.

3

WRITING A TRAINING MAP

Jerry had convinced a hospital staff to purchase a new heart-monitoring machine from his company, but the hospital insisted that the deal include a training guide for teaching people to use the machine. Jerry's company had no training department and assigned the task to him as part of the sales package. Jerry knew a lot about selling the machine, and he knew that the hospital wanted the manual so that it could conduct in-house training on the use of the machine. Jerry had always wanted to be a writer, and he was a good salesman, so he assumed that he could apply his sales pitches to the writing process.

However, he was not sure where or how to begin writing. Finally, one of his co-workers advised, "Start with an outline."

"Yeah, yeah," was Jerry's response. He thought to himself, "Outlines are boring. I want to see where my writing will take me—that's what makes writing an adventure." He remembered, though, that he had seen an outline of the history of the heart-monitoring machine. He decided to begin his training guide with this history, and this is what he wrote:

> Doctors have been monitoring the heart since Egyptian and Greek times when they first put their ears to their patients' chests. In 1866, Laennec invented the stethoscope. The next big leap in heart-monitoring technology came with the invention of the computer and new ways to record heart patterns. Our product offers the latest refinement in measuring and recording several heart functions.

Jerry got excited about the machine's history. He thought about turning it into a slide show—perhaps even a prerecorded slide show for the hospital's convenience. If this were not possible, Jerry thought that someone could make overhead transparencies with sketches of these important historical moments. But he realized that his lone paragraph did not provide enough material for a slide show. Wondering what to do, he remembered a couple of stories that he had heard about the heart-monitoring machines. He had used one in his sales pitch and he thought that the other was entertaining, so he added them to his training guide:

> One of the patients was on our machine while she had her appendix out. Because of the machine, the doctors noticed some unusual fluctuations of her heart, and they were able to change her medication and save her life right in the middle of the operation. That shows you how important this machine is.

"That will make them feel good about using this machine," Jerry reflected. He decided that slides of operations could be included or that the words "Saved patient's life" could be flashed onto the screen. Then he recorded several other stories, some of which would be good for a laugh.

Jerry submitted his new training guide to the hospital and was surprised when the hospital rejected it. The only feedback the hospital gave him was one question: "Where's the learning objective?" Jerry was puzzled because he thought that his training guide made the objective—teaching people about the machine—obvious. "I shouldn't have to spell out the objective," he argued.

Jerry made many mistakes that better planning and writing could have prevented. He did not understand the objective of training; therefore, he did not know that he had not reached it. Jerry needed benchmarks during the writing process to keep him focused and to indicate whether the training manual was likely to be successful when implemented. A well-written map could have steered Jerry away from his entertaining but useless guide.

Effective planning is essential to the creation of useful and practical training materials. The planning process should at least include preparation of a list of topics or skills and of an objective. Additional planning can include the preparation of outlines, background audience information, an estimated program length, a list of materials needed, program objectives. The objectives should be behavioral, observable, and measurable; that is, they should reflect behavior, not attitudes or emotions.

These preparatory steps may seem time consuming and unnecessary to some. However, putting a training map in writing not only benefits the writer, but it contributes in some way to the design. A list or outline guides the writing of more detailed training information. Keeping the map posted during the writing will steer the writing in the right direction; it will also be more efficient. Having objectives will help to ensure that the parts add up to a whole that truly satisfies the training needs.

The training map can communicate the writer's overview and goals for the project. This tends to smooth the process of delegation and parceling out of work. In addition, the training map can serve as a proposal for possible clients. It is a way to say, "This is what I have in mind; what do you think?"—which can save time.

The training map can also help if the client, having seen the original proposal, says, "That's not what I wanted." The map makes it easy to add, delete, or change the program. The same holds true for communications with supervisors. People who assign projects do not always communicate their wants and needs clearly; they also may think of new ideas when they see the initial proposal. If either the client or the supervisor agrees to the proposal without changes, of course, the trainer will be able to proceed without further delays. If one or the other agrees, it is wise to obtain a written agreement to the training program. This is not to say that changes cannot be made or that creativity will not be permitted. Trainers can always renegotiate for the inclusion of additional elements.

CHOOSING A FOCUS

This book refers to the preparatory writing as a *map*. Others may call it an *outline*, a *treatment*, a *design*, a *program development work sheet*, or a *course planner*. Whatever its name, its purpose is to help solve an organizational problem through training. The research and the needs assessment most likely uncovered problems, because training designers usually are not asked to do research if problems do not exist. What the trainer needs to do is to focus on the most pressing problem or to plan a series of training programs. The purpose of training programs is to solve problems, not simply to make the symptoms go away. To ensure that the training will solve the problem, the training designer should conduct an analysis of the causes of the problem.

The start of the process should be a brainstorming session. Do not censor any thoughts or ideas that come to mind; write them all down. At first, write in nonlinear lists: start with a major idea, write it in the center of the page, and surround it with other ideas. Next, cluster related ideas by circling them or by drawing connecting lines. This produces an illustration of how ideas relate; it may also reveal some extraneous parts that can be discarded. For example, Figure 3-1 gives some problems revealed by research at a restaurant.

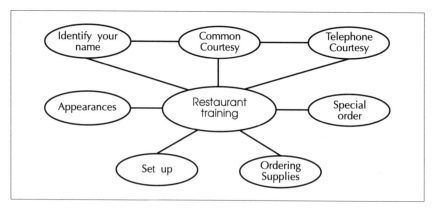

Figure 3-1. Sample Nonlinear List

In this case, the training designer chose to begin with an emphasis on interpersonal skills and had a plan for addressing other topics at a later time. Another method of brainstorming is to jot ideas on cards. Sort and arrange them in different ways until some sort of logical order emerges; some cards can often be discarded at this time. Writing criteria, such as "costs" or "highest needs" and using a system of numbering or pluses and minuses will help to weed out all but the most critical topics. The process of prioritizing training needs is not merely for the sake of organization; it will make a difference in the actual training sessions as well. A training program that addresses every issue causes information overload, which tends to confuse people and eventually causes them to tune out. Cramming leaves less room in the program for repetition of important points and questions. Ultimately, an overcrowded agenda is a waste of time, because the audience will retain very little of what they have learned.

It will often be the case that not all of the people need all of the training, which can further complicate the selection and prioritization process. For example, a trainer assesses the need for secretarial training within an organization. The trainer conducts research and interviews and concludes that there are four core secretarial skills: telephone skills, word-processing skills, filing skills, and memo- and letter-writing skills. The trainer prepares the following list of statistics after speaking to the organization's twelve secretaries:

- *Telephone:* ten are skilled; two could do better;
- *Word processing:* two are skilled;
- *Filing:* ten are skilled;
- *Writing memos and letters:* seven are skilled.

Although all four skills are essential to a good secretary's repertoire and although not all secretaries possess all four skills, there is one area in which skills are particularly lacking: word processing. Therefore, this is the area of most importance and should be the focus of the training.

OUTLINES AND FLOW CHARTS

Once a focal topic has been selected through the brainstorming and listing activities, the training designer must organize his or her presentation of the process. The outline is more sophisticated than the list because the outline depicts relationships between general topics and their subtopics. Arrangement of the outline is a matter of personal preference. Figure 3-2 gives a sample process outline.

Outline for Floor Cleaning
  I. Gather materials
       A. Broom and dust
       B. Mop
       C. Water (in bucket)
       D. Cleanser, measured
 II. Sweep open areas, then closets and
           smaller rooms
III. Mop to strip floor
       A. Degree of saturation
       B. Rubbing techniques
       C. Judging cleanliness
 IV. Using Buffer
       A. Adding wax
       B. Holding handle
       C. Proper strokes
       D. Measuring doneness

Figure 3-2. Sample Process Outline

Outlines also show the order in which steps occur. The order can be determined by the nature of the job (the above floor-cleaning outline depicts a start-to-finish task that leaves little room for alteration). Sometimes the process starts with more difficult tasks in order to provide for practice and repetition of skills. Beginning with more elementary skills is a good way to bolster trainees' confidence; it also provides the opportunity to add building blocks of more complex skills as the trainees master each level.

Still more sophisticated is the flow chart. Flow charts are more complex than outlines in that they not only depict order but also offer options. A training map constructed as a flow chart could require the trainer to make choices. For example, the training designer may wish to introduce a new concept but does not know whether the trainer will have access to audiovisual equipment. Therefore, an option is built into the training design. For example:

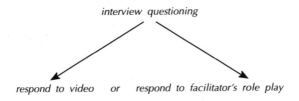

Another purpose of the flow chart is to provide another person who will be conducting the training program with options: "Give your own example here or use this one" or "Use one of these two learning activities." For example:

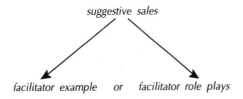

The training program could even be a self-study guide in which the trainees make choices based on whether they want to learn more about certain topics or whether they wish to move to a new topic. Robert Mager (1962) uses this technique in his books.

Other ways of mapping training besides flow charts and outlines can be used. Patricia McLagan (1978) uses circles to symbolize concepts, triangles to symbolize learners' observations, rectangles to symbolize learning experiences, and diamonds to symbolize on-the-job actions. Be creative— make up symbols to suit your needs and writing style.

ADDITIONAL PLANNING STEPS

Others may find it helpful if the training map includes other information about the training program, particularly if the map may turn into a contract of agreement. If the map might become a contract, it is important to spell out needs regarding time, resources, and people involved.

Time Needs

Estimate the length of the program and the time that it will take to develop it. Break the estimates into increments if possible, which will help in budgeting time and giving presenters adequate notice to prepare. If, in the earlier example, Jerry had bothered to estimate the length of his program, he would have known whether or not he had enough material to fill a program.

Resource Needs

Some time will be needed for researching and purchasing programs or for developing in-house materials such as videotapes. The program budget will dictate what and how much to purchase. Be sure to list available and needed equipment (e.g, previous programs, materials, studio, word processors, and graphics machines). Another important resource is people. Behind-the-scenes people may include typists, graphic artists, and producers. A resource list may look something like the following:

Resources
Development Time: 120 hours @ $30/hour
Facilitation Time: 40 hours @ $25/hour
Meeting-Room Rental: 5 days @ $100/day
Purchased Video: $325

People Needs

It is important to consider the people who will assist the training designer: co-designers, decision-makers, facilitators, and trainees. Consultants hired by outside organizations will want to identify the decision makers at the outset. It is more difficult to list the in-house decision makers. Training designers should answer the following questions:

1. Who asked that the program be implemented?
2. Who saw the need for training?
3. Who has the power to influence whether and how the program will be administered?
4. Who will be presenting the program that you are writing?

For example, Jerry should have known that supervising nurses would be the hospital's trainers. One will often write differently for professional trainers than for managers, supervisors, or line workers, all of whom may be presenting a training program for the first time. Keep the presenters in mind while writing; be sure that they will be able to follow the guide as intended.

The most important people, of course, are the audience. They are the targets of the training—the destination at the end of the training map. Find out about members of the audience; make sure that you know the answers to the following questions:

1. How old are they?

2. What are their jobs?

3. How long have they been with the organizations and in their respective departments?

4. What professional experience and backgrounds do they have?

5. Are they women, men, or a mixed group?

6. Do they belong to any minority groups?

7. What special needs, hopes, or fears might they have about this training program?

8. What other training programs have they been through? Is the other training related to the training program that you will be conducting?

9. Try to picture two or three of these trainees in your mind and write the program to and for them. Imagine them reading over your shoulder. Will your writing make sense to them when the presenter reads it?

10. What are they doing after they leave your seminar?

The answers to these ten questions will shape and guide the formation of the training program.

OBJECTIVES

It is important to establish training objectives in advance. Picture the trainees before and after the training program. In what ways have they changed? What are they doing differently? This exercise will help to clarify the objectives (what the trainer wants to accomplish) of the program. Objectives evolve directly from needs assessments. Try to limit major objectives to one general statement. If objectives are too complicated, training will be difficult.

The statement of objectives will take the following form:

Audience   -   Action verb   -   Measurable criteria

Begin the statement with the audience. Refer to the audience as trainees, participants, managers, nurses, new employees—whatever term is most appropriate. Follow it with an action verb that describes what the trainees will be doing on the job or what they should be learning to do. Remember that verbs such as *know, learn,* and *see* describe actions that others cannot observe. The action verb should describe an action that can be observed and measured. We can observe and measure body language and spoken or written thoughts. State the objective in positive terms; it is more difficult to observe what someone is *not* doing than it is to observe what someone *is* doing. Use verbs such as *identify, define, use, name,* and *repair.*

Good statements of objectives are not only behavioral and observable but measurable as well. The following objective statement is behavioral and observable but not measurable: "Cashiers will fill out refund slips accurately." It is difficult to measure accuracy, as this requires individual judgment. Instead of using "accurately," one could state that "Cashiers will fill out refund slips correctly 100 percent of the time" or that "Cashiers will answer at least 95 percent of a series of questions regarding refund-slip processing correctly." In addition, one must define accuracy. Is accuracy completeness, or does it mean that math is calculated correctly? In other words, the more measurable the objective, the easier it will be to prove during an evaluation that the training had a positive effect.

Training designers should also prepare statements of objectives to direct the progress of the training program. In-progress or enabling objectives guide the presenters and keep them on track. Writers of training materials formulate these objectives by taking the concepts and points from the outline or flow chart and writing them up as behavioral, measurable objectives.

CHAPTER SUMMARY

Mapping the training process serves as an outline for later writing and shows others how the program will be developed. Free-form, nonlinear writing can help the training designer to focus on concepts and skills for the training program. Outlines, flow charts, and symbols can be used to illustrate the program's sequence and available options. It is also important to find out what time, resources, and people will be available for the program. Above all, it is important to formulate objectives—a general objective to show where the program is going and interim objectives to show how to get there.

REFERENCES

Mager, R.F. (1962). *Preparing instructional objectives.* Palo Alto, CA: Fearon Publishers.
McLagan, P.A. (1978). *Helping others learn: Designing programs for adults.* Reading, MA: Addison-Wesley.

4

WRITING THE DETAILED DESIGN

Lee, a training designer, wanted to design a program to train various bank branch managers to make recruiting presentations. These managers would visit job fairs, schools, and various organizations to talk to groups about the benefits of working for Franklin Financial. Members of the personnel department would do the training.

Lee had researched the audiences, the selling points of Franklin, and the needs of the branch managers, who had had little or no experience in giving presentations. She formulated objectives and a brief outline. Then she decided to elaborate the outline. Her supervisor advised her to use some jazzy titles and phrases to help the presenters remember what to say. She created Figure 4-1.

Lee also planned some learning activities in which the managers would practice making the presentations and would role play answering the questions. Unfortunately, when the personnel department members presented this program, they lost the managers' attention. The managers had not felt confident about making presentations to begin with, and all the caveats shook their confidence even more.

Unfortunately, the personnel department did not know what the titles in the presentation meant. For example, what did "action auction" mean? One staff member thought it referred to the charity auction to which Franklin contributed annually. Another thought it meant that Franklin has no ties with auctioneers, and still another used auctioning

How to Make a Recruiting Presentation

Objective: Managers will give a 45-minute presentation about Franklin Financial to persuade at least one person to apply for a job with Franklin.

Materials:
Overhead slides: Agenda; Don'ts
Slides of line graphs: Comparison with competition; Franklin's growth
Video: Franklin commercial
Benefits package handouts

Training Procedure:
Starting out:

- Don't discriminate against minorities.
- Don't use offensive language.
- Don't say "he" when you mean "he or she."
- Don't promise them something we can't give them.
- Don't keep your voice too soft.
- Don't just read notes.

Then go through the main steps of the presentation:

- Introduce yourself.
- Describe Franklin's fine points: give an overview of Franklin.
- Action auction: sell them on Franklin.
- Contend with the competition: make comparisons.
- Job jamboree
- Company climate
- Customer congratulations
- Success ladder
- Benefit battle
- Requirements

Finally, tell the presenters to ask for questions.

Figure 4-1. Lee's Elaborated Outline

as an analogy for how loan officers deal with realtors. Lee had intended the "action auction" to be an analogy for the managers to use to sell the audience on working at Franklin, but she had obviously not gotten her point across. The personnel presenters also did not understand the other expressions. They could not explain them, and Lee offered no examples.

In the training sessions, the presenters spent most of the time going over the benefits package, because it was a subject with which they were familiar. Potential employees did not perceive the presentation as an advertisement for Franklin Federal, because no opportunity for touting the bank occurred.

The only recruitment consisted of the managers' talking about themselves and their careers, because they were familiar topics. The managers were even less informed than the personnel department as to the meaning of the slogans and were therefore unable to illustrate them with examples. As a result, the presentation scared away more applicants than it attracted, and Franklin Federal began to receive negative publicity.

Lee's design needed a stimulating introduction, a thorough explanation of the concepts and skills needed to make presentations, and illustrative examples with each point. If she intended them to use visual aides, she could have helped the presenters know when to use them and how to transition in and out of them. Written summaries would have prevented the trainers from having to make them up on the spot.

Of course, experienced trainers who are familiar with the subject matter may only need objectives and an outline. However, a detailed script will increase the chances that the training will be successful and that each trainer who conducts the program will do so in a similarly consistent manner.

Think of the training design as the script for a play. Create a motivating beginning (a mind grabber) to enliven the introduction. State the depth to which trainers will explain the skills and concepts. Supply examples and transitions from one step to another. Finally, suggest a summary. Good writing skills will enable the training designer to customize a purchased training program to a specific organization.

WRITING INTRODUCTIONS

An introduction sets the stage for the training program. It should include a mind grabber, an agenda, a statement about the purpose or reason for the program, and a reference to the learning activities. Sometimes an icebreaker activity that introduces participants to one another is appropriate. The parts of the introduction can occur in any order. Experiment with order; try to discover which order best prepares the audience for what follows. Label the introduction and its parts for the trainers.

The Mind Grabber

The mind grabber helps participants to make the transition from work, home, or whatever activity with which they were involved before the training session began. A mind-grabber acts like a beckoning finger, enticing the audience to want to learn more.

Mind grabbers can take many forms. They can be startling (something that the participants did not know or something that contradicts common sense). A statistic or story can serve the same purpose. For example, a training program for social workers who deal with the elderly could start with the statement: "Abuse of aging parents is increasing. Last year, 40,000 cases were reported"; or for a nutrition class: "Decaffeinated coffee can be harmful because of the chemicals used to take out the caffeine. In one experiment, scientists fed caffeinated and decaffeinated coffee grounds to worms, and all of the worms in the decaffeinated grounds died."

A similar story could present a worst-case scenario. The worst-case scenario is developed by asking the following question: What goes wrong when the skills are not used? Or conversely, what is the ideal case? What are the consequences when all goes well using these skills? Any of these could be exaggerated so that they are humorous and provoke laughter. Guard against being too negative or singling out individuals; these, like Lee's list of don'ts, can turn off the audience. Similarly, a thought-provoking question catches the audience's attention. This type of question is usually rhetorical and does not require the audience's immediate response. For example: Would you rather have claims filled out quickly or completely? Which do you think saves the company more money?

Mind grabbers can also take the form of videos (Chapter 7 discusses the writing of videoscripts in more detail). Overhead slides, which can function as mind grabbers, can illustrate statistics with graphs and charts. Role playing can also function as mind grabbers. For example, a trainer may role play the part of a manager speaking to a new employee. In the plan, write out exactly what the trainer is to say and how he or she is to say it; also include stage directions (see Figure 4-2).

Objectives

A good introduction also tells the participants the purpose or objective of the training program. Use a simple statement to make the transition between the mind grabber and the objective. For example: "The answer to this problem/question....To avoid this or attain this,...." The introduction should set forth the major objective. Because "objective" is more of a training term, the trainer will need either to define the word or to substitute a word, such as "goal" or "purpose," with which the audience may be more familiar. For example: "The purpose of this program is to teach you to fill

Directions: Walk up to one of the participants and address just that person as if you are that person's supervisor.

Trainer: Before I explain any of your tasks, I'm going to walk with you through the department and introduce you to all the other employees. I don't expect you to remember their names, but this will let them know who you are and what job you have.

Figure 4-2. Sample Script from Training Design

out forms correctly and thoroughly" or "Our goal today is to teach you the importance of choosing foods that are low in cholesterol."

It is important to tell the audience why they should learn what they are about to be taught. Some presenters prefer to start the program with a statement of objectives rather than with the mind grabber. Beginning the program with the objective tells the audience exactly what is in store for them and may even state the purpose of the mind grabber. Starting with the objective rather than with the mind grabber also can remove the surprise and build-up that hook an audience. Each trainer must decide which approach is best suited to each individual training situation.

WRITING THE AGENDA

Just as mapping helps training designers, the agenda serves to guide the participants through the skills or concepts being taught in the program. List the agenda items in the training design and also suggest some ways for the trainer to refer to the agenda items and for the trainer to relate those agenda items to the program objectives (see Figure 4-3).

Agenda:
   Review
   Code Checking
   Unit Testing
   System Testing

   Trainer: Because we all want to be better programmers, we'll start out with a basic review and then go on to trouble shooting. We'll take you through three ways to look for bugs and then give you a chance to try them out. *Code checking* is a logical exercise. *Unit testing* tests the program against the data that you expect it to manipulate. *System testing* lets you implement the program and see whether it throws off anything that you didn't expect.

Figure 4-3. Sample Agenda and Ways to Relate Items to Program Objectives

Set the trainees up for what they will be doing, particularly if they have never attended a workshop before or if they are accustomed to passively listening to lectures. Note in the design for the trainer to remind participants to take notes, to speak up, and to participate in role plays or any other planned learning activities. The design may specify that the trainer tell participants in advance about the learning activities, or that the trainer pique participants' interest by alluding to activities without completely describing them (see Figure 4-4).

   Trainer: This session is going to be a little different from the lectures that you remember from school. You won't just be sitting quietly while I talk. You all know a lot, so you'll have a chance to share your experiences. You will also have opportunities to try out new skills. This will allow you to practice without the pressure of being on the job; it will also help you remember what to do back at work.

Figure 4-4. Sample for Setting Up Trainees

ICEBREAKERS

Another part of the training design is the introduction of the trainees to one another. The simplest method is to allow the participants to introduce themselves, one at a time. The objective is to help them to feel comfortable about speaking to the group. After giving an explanation, as illustrated in Figure 4-5, the trainer should call on members one at a time and encourage them to talk about themselves.

Books such as *The Encyclopedia of Icebreakers* (Forbess-Greene, 1983), the *Structured Experience Kit* (Pfeiffer & Jones 1983), and *Games Trainers Play* (Newstrom & Scannel, 1980) are excellent sources of icebreakers.

Even if all the participants are acquainted with one another, the introduction phase can be regarded as an opportunity for the participants to discover new things about one another—especially things related to the topic of the training program. Furthermore, studies indicate that people who speak in front of the group once are more likely to speak up again. An icebreaker activity is a perfect way of having everyone speak at the beginning of the session.

WRITING EXPLANATIONS

At this point, the training designer has chosen the concepts, skills, or job tasks that trainers must learn. Now, the designer must indicate to the trainers how he or she wishes to present them. The introduction provides an overview of the sequence of the presentation, with a goal of making the trainees more knowledgeable and competent in the skills presented. This can be accomplished only if the trainees *understand* and *remember* what they are taught. The job of the training designer is to create an atmosphere most conducive to understanding and remembering. Trainers must give an explanation of a new or misunderstood skill or

> **Facilitator:** I'd like you to introduce yourselves. Tell a little about your background and how long you've been with the company. I'll start. My name is_____, and I've worked here _____ years.

Figure 4-5. Sample Icebreaker

process before employees try to implement the process or skill on their own.

It is most helpful to create learning activities and handouts *at the same time* as the explanations. It is difficult to tell whether training developers have written an adequate explanation unless they can coordinate them with the learning activities and handouts. Designing both at the same time also forces the writer to keep the audience in mind. This book separates each topic into a different chapter simply to keep the different types of required writing skills separate.

Several techniques of constructing explanations help the learners understand and remember what they are told. The primary ones are *definitions, literary devices, examples,* and *pictures.*

Definitions

When explaining a skill or process, try to think of all the questions a new employee might have, and answer them. This ensures that trainers relate what trainees need to know in the simplest possible way. This is the key to writing clear, thorough definitions. Definitions for training purposes should not be abstract, dictionary-style definitions; rather, they should be descriptions of *how things work.* It is important to ensure that each learner is learning the same material. The word "car" brings images of sports cars to some and station wagons to others. Clearly, "car" is not specific enough to ensure that all listeners will envision the same type of automobile. Think of the journalist's "W" (who, what, where, when, why) questions during this step. What is it? How do employees do it? Why do they do it that way? When should they do it, with whom, and where?

State the definition in two or three concise sentences. State what the skill or idea is, why it is important, and how it works. For example, you might tell the trainer: When you're using an open-ended probe, you're saying "Tell me more." That gets the speaker to open up.

The definition can also include criteria or performance standards; this will enable the trainees to evaluate their understanding and implementation of the concepts or skills. Accordingly, the definition should not only state how the skill fits into the bigger picture of departmental or organizational goals; it should also state how using the skill will benefit each person. A sample definition is presented in Figure 4-6.

> *Mirroring* is the technique of stating to someone your interpretation of what he or she has said to you. This technique allows the person to know what you perceive that he or she said; if your perception is not correct, the person can help you to understand what he or she is trying to say. If you want to get ahead as a manager, you need to be a good listener. Mirroring is especially effective when the other person is expressing strong emotions, because it helps to keep him or her from becoming defensive or overly emotional.

Figure 4-6. Sample Definition

Trainers must make sure that they define not only the main concepts but any other jargon or work-specific language that could be new to the audience. Example: We'll be using the word "flats" to refer to four-by-four foot fixtures without shelves.

Literary Devices

Literary devices (analogies, metaphors, similes, allegories, acronyms, alliteration, and mnemonic devices) create mental pictures out of words that help to relate the unfamiliar to the familiar.

An *analogy* compares one thing to another. Learners are better able to remember new information if they can connect it to something with which they are familiar. For example, the trainer might use the following analogy:

> Giving a learner too many points at once is like the use of telephones during a disaster. When a large number of people try to use the telephone system at once, the system cannot handle them; it either shuts down or lets only a few calls through. Similarly, an inexperienced person will not learn anything or will only pick up a few points because of the overload.

Metaphors and similes are types of analogies. A metaphor describes a noun by calling it something else ("When the deadline approaches, I turn into a hurricane"), whereas a simile uses the word *like* to make a comparison ("A computer is like a typewriter; much of the keyboard is the same.") Analogies are effective only if the comparison is obvious and if the parallelism is evident.

Allegories offer more elaborate analogies, but they require a good deal of creativity to create. An allegory tells a fable or parable; Blanchard and Johnson's (1983) one-minute-manager parable is one of the best known in the field of human resource development. Byham and Cox (1989) use a story about "zapping" to explain empowerment. Allegories often begin with "Once upon a time" or "In the beginning."

While analogies help explain parts of explanations, *acronyms* can help people remember the names of the parts and their order. When creating an acronym, experiment with the steps or concepts that will be taught to see if they can spell something. They are often used to help people remember what they have learned. For example, many one-time pianists are familiar with the expression *Every Good Boy Does Fine*. The first letters of each word represent the five keys in the treble clef. Most science students are apt to learn the acronym *Roy G. Biv,* each letter of which stands for a color in the spectrum: red, orange, yellow, green, blue, indigo, and violet. Telephone training could begin with an introduction to GINA:

> **G**reet
> **I**dentify yourself
> **N**ame (use the customer's name)
> **A**sk to assist.

A cartoon of a telephone as a woman's head, GINA Telephone, helps trainees to remember.

Alliteration is a helpful memory jogger in that each concept begins with the same letter. For example:

The 3 L's of Leadership
- **L**ight the way with a vision.
- **L**ift your employees out of their ordinary lives.
- **L**et them participate.

Be as simple and as brief as possible when writing explanations that incorporate literary devices. Use language familiar to the trainers and learners; define any unfamiliar terms. Pay attention to word choice. Certain words have negative connotations that could offend some and be misconstrued by others. For example, "drugs" has a very different connotation than "medications," and the use of "drugs" for "medications" could be distracting or offensive to medical personnel.

Examples

Another way to help learners remember is by using examples. Examples not only specify an idea, they also provide a mental model for action. Some trainers can easily think up examples; others can be inspired by examples provided by the training designer. Ideas for examples often present themselves during the research phase. Be prepared to add examples from the organization to customize a purchased program and to make it more relevant to the participants. When they hear a job-specific example, some participants may argue that that could never happen in their plant or office. It sometimes is better to use nonjob-related examples that will not entangle the participants with the accuracy of the rest of the example. If the job is to train bank tellers in customer service, use shoe salespeople as examples. If the explanation is how to negotiate with two conflicting employees, use a parent-and-children example. The important points will still be made, but the learners will not be distracted.

Experiment with internal and external examples. Write the example in story form so that trainers can understand the examples and put them in their own words. Every major idea in the program should be illustrated with an example; this will satisfy both the abstract and concrete ways that people think and assimilate information. For example, a training designer writing a program for a water-safety course might create a short vignette like the one in Figure 4-7.

For example, one lifeguard noticed a lack of movement in one part of the pool. He quickly dived in and rescued a swimmer with a head injury. This illustrates why it is important to stay alert to people's movements in a pool.

Figure 4-7. Sample of an Example

Do not become frustrated and stuck if examples do not come to mind while writing the explanations. Simply note the location of the examples in the text. Concentrate on examples after completing each section of text. Then come back to the text and insert the examples.

Format

The format used to write explanations is important. A combination of an outline and a script often is easiest to read. Use headings, subheadings, italics, or underlining to make important points stand out. The format should help the reader to locate main parts of the text quickly; it also should alert the trainer when to use audiovisual equipment.

VISUAL AIDS

Analogies and verbal examples instruct the trainer in what to say. But they do not tell the trainer what to *do*. The training designer must also prepare the facilitator to lead the audience from activity to activity and to direct the audience's attention from place to place or topic to topic. It is not enough for a trainer to say, "Watch this," when instructing participants to look at a diagram or watch a video. The trainer needs to guide the learners in how to watch and what skills to look for. For example, the training designer may want the trainer to show a still picture. A still picture could be an overhead transparency, a projected photo slide, or a poster. The designer's job is to choose or design the audiovisual aids. It is best to make a checklist of all audiovisual aids needed for the trainer. The checklist should also appear in the lesson plan to ensure that the trainer uses the audiovisual aids at the proper places in the program. It is also important for visual aids to have distinctive titles.

The training designer has the option of incorporating an audiotape or videotape of an executive, an expert in the field, or a celebrity explaining a particular topic. The program could also include guest speakers or panel discussions. If feasible, these can add variety and interest to the program and take some of the speaking burden away from the presenter. The training designer may be responsible for arranging these extras. At the least, the designer should suggest topics in the design. At most, the training designer will write the expert's or panel's speeches.

Often, demonstrations of tasks or processes are the most effective methods of explanation. On-site demonstrations, videotapes, or audiotapes can depict skills in action for participants to absorb and imitate. Videotapes are especially helpful for demonstrating skills that involve machines or settings that cannot be brought into the training session. They also add variety. Again, training designers should write introductions so that the trainer knows to direct the audience's attention to watch or listen.

Trainers themselves sometimes demonstrate skills or processes. Sometimes, they operate the machine or use the product; other times, they may role play. If the designer wishes the trainer to role play, he or she should be sure to write a script complete with stage directions. Figure 4-8 demonstrates such a script.

Necktie-Knotting Demonstration

Trainer: First pick up the right side like this. Next, make a loop and hold it this way.... *(Directions:* Tie knot as you explain each part.)

Suggestive-Selling Role Play

Trainer: Let's say the customer says no to my suggestion of purchasing additional vacuum cleaner attachments. *(Directions:* Move to a different position to show that you are assuming the role of the salesperson. Address one of the participants as if he or she were the customer.) I understand that you don't want any of these attachments now. I'm sure that after you've used this wonderful machine a while you will want the window-cleaning attachment. Here's my card, and I'll be back next week to show you how it works.

Figure 4-8. Sample Demonstration Script

Audiovisual aids and examples provide pictures and sounds of the way that skills and processes work. People are better able to recall what they have learned if the training appealed to more than one of their senses. Try to design the training program to appeal to as many as possible. This also provides the designer with options. It is easier to be creative if one has access to an audiocassette player, a flip chart, and a videocassette recorder than if one is limited to a flip chart.

WRITING TRANSITIONS

Transitions bridge parts of the training program. They lead from one concept to another or in and out of examples or visual aids. For example, the transition from a visual aid back to the program often takes the form of a learning activity such as a discussion question. Construct transitions by repeating or summarizing what was just said, then relate that to the upcoming portion of the program (see Figure 4-9).

Trainer: We've discussed how to fill in the first side of an accident report. That's relatively straightforward because each part of the report is labeled. The second side is more difficult to fill out because it's open-ended. You'll need to record exactly what happened, so let's talk about how to do that.

Figure 4-9. Sample Transition

Without this transition, the program may not flow smoothly; the trainers may lose the train of thought; or the trainer may move too abruptly from one part of the program to another.

WRITING THE SUMMARY

A complete summary included in the training design will help the trainer to wind down the program and to conclude the session on an upbeat, motivating note. The summary should repeat the main points of the program and any additional points that came up in the meeting. It should remind the trainees to use the skills and tell them how to do follow-up. Figure 4-10 presents a sample summary.

How to Use a Laminating Machine

(*Directions:* Show diagram 1, the laminating machine, again.)

1. Let's review all the steps we've talked about for using the laminator. First, you'll turn it on by pressing this button and waiting at least two minutes until it has heated.

2. Next, turn on the pressure, and here's how you test for pressure. (Explain.)

3. Third, line up your copy on the plastic and run it through while you make it smooth, but also be careful not to get burned.

(*Trainer:* Add any additional uses of the laminator that the audience has mentioned.)

Figure 4-10. Sample Summary

The trainees should leave feeling not only that they know the skills but that they will be able to use them. The training designer may want to formulate an action plan or post-assignment for trainees to use on the job. Many training sessions offer a follow-up session to reinforce the skills, to answer any questions that the trainees might have, and to check progress. A follow-up session also allows participants to give the trainer feedback on the effectiveness and applicability of his or her training. The designer should outline the content of the follow-up session if one is desired.

CHAPTER SUMMARY

A typical detailed design will contain the following components:

- Objectives
- Introduction
- Definitions
- Examples
- Audiovisual aids
- Transitions
- Summary

Writing a detailed explanation in script form increases the training designer's chances that his or her program will be properly delivered and helpful to the program participants. A thorough script leaves less to chance than an outline or training map. A well-written introduction helps the trainer to excite the audience about learning and prepares them for what will follow. Carefully crafted definitions that describe processes and skills, combined with literary devices such as analogies, allegories, and acronyms, enhance learning by engaging trainees' senses and previous experiences and contribute to retention of learning. Effective transitions and a thorough summary contribute to the program's continuity and completeness while adding professional polish.

REFERENCES

Blanchard, K., & Johnson, S. (1983). *The one minute manager.* New York: William Morrow.

Byham, W.C., & Cox, J. (1989). *Zapp! The lightning of empowerment.* (Available from University Associates, San Diego, CA.)

Forbess-Greene, S. (1983). *The encyclopedia of icebreakers.* San Diego, CA: University Associates.

Newstrom, J., & Scannell, E.E. (1980). *Games trainers play.* New York: McGraw-Hill.

Pfeiffer, J.W., & Jones, J.E. (Eds.). (1983). *Structured experience kit.* San Diego, CA: University Associates.

5

WRITING LEARNING ACTIVITIES

Joe, a training designer for a government agency, designed a program to teach disaster preparedness to county and city employees. His program was intended not for departments that would be called upon for aid in the event of a disaster (such as the public works or police force) but for other government employees who would themselves be victims if a disaster struck. The plan was for each department head to make the presentation along with a member of the training department.

Joe researched the program carefully. He consulted with building inspectors about the safety of each government building, and he surveyed a sample of employees from each department to find out what they already knew about disaster preparedness. The employees seemed to know little about preparation, escape routes, or how to handle the panic and chaos that would be part of an emergency situation.

Joe's research provided him with some specific objectives. The main objective of his program was to ensure that the employees could handle a disaster calmly and that they would be safe. Joe created a training map for disaster preparedness that included such steps as stocking batteries, bottled water, and flashlights; and locating gas-line switches and fuse boxes. He wanted the employees to know the locations of safe places in their buildings and the best routes for escape. In drawing up these plans, Joe considered the effects of earthquakes, high winds, floods, and fires. Joe wrote a detailed script that included many examples, visual aids, and some dramatic audiotapes and videotapes. He worked with technicians to simulate a disaster, which would act as the mind grabber for the beginning of the program. The technicians created a way to make a loud boom, whose vibration would feel like an earthquake or explosion, and to turn off the lights simultaneously. Joe hoped that this opening would generate a bit of fear and that it would convince the audience that they needed to know what to do. The first page of Joe's leader's guide is presented in Figure 5-1.

Joe went on to design each part of the program. He had an audiotape of the governor's speech about disasters, which he edited to help the trainer emphasize important points. He obtained a fire extinguisher and a model of a gas valve for the trainer to use in demonstrations. He wrote detailed descriptions of everything the trainer should say and do. He found newsreels of hurricanes, earthquakes, and other natural disasters that illustrated both the worst that could happen and how ordinary people handled the situation. Joe included maps of many of the government buildings for the trainer to display. He wrote instructions for the trainer to discuss escape routes and tell the audience to avoid the elevators during a fire. The last section of Joe's program dealt with teaching breathing techniques and how to focus on immediate needs in the event of a disaster.

For all of this painstaking preparation, Joe forgot one critical element of the training program: he failed to include audience response in the training design. Joe set his audience up to be passive. They would not speak; they would not write; and they would not touch any of the equipment. The trainers told Joe how easy his program was to read and follow because it was so detailed and well written. The trainers knew exactly what to do. They believed that the variety and vivid examples would hold the audience's attention.

After the disaster training was conducted, Joe received further accolades. Many employees told him how much

Introduction

Objective: Employees will acknowledge their need to learn what to do in the event of a disaster.

Trainer: Welcome to our program on disaster preparedness.

Directions: Turn on sound; lights go out.

Trainer: (feigning fear) Oh no! What's happening?

(pause as audience reacts)

Lights go on again.

Trainer: We just gave you a taste of some of the things that could occur in a disaster. Would *you* know what to do?

(Trainer: show chart of agenda)

Goal: To handle a disaster calmly.

- Prepare

- Equipment and supplies

- How to evacuate

- How to stay calm

Trainer: The purpose of this program is to make sure that you know what to do in a disaster. We're concerned about your safety, so we want you to take care of yourselves if a disaster ever strikes. We're going to show you some ways to prepare, then we'll tell you what to do with things like fire extinguishers and gas valves. The most important thing you'll want to know is how to evacuate. Finally, we have some tips for you on staying calm.

Figure 5-1. First Page of Joe's Leader's Guide

they appreciated seeing all the disasters and said that the program was exciting and stimulating. However, a visiting fire inspector asked the employees about the training. They praised the program, but when the fire inspector asked what they had learned, they were not able to remember.

A few weeks after the final training session, a chemical spill caused a fire in one of the government buildings. The employees nearest the fire poured water on the flames, causing them to spread. They were unable to figure out how to use the fire extinguisher. One employee found the gas valve, but instead of turning it off, he turned it up so that gas leaked and further fueled the fire.

At least ten minutes passed before anyone called the fire department—everyone thought that someone else had already called. No one could remember whom to contact in the building. As a result, the fire alarm was not activated until the fire was almost out of control. Most people panicked. Many filled the elevators, others crowded and pushed to descend the stairs, while still others tried to rescue people and belongings.

Because of the lack of preparation, almost one-third of the people in the building were injured. The disaster-preparedness training had failed because people did not remember or use the information that was presented at the training session. They could not remember or use what they had been told because they had not had a chance to practice with the equipment and to rehearse the procedures that they had been taught. Obviously, Joe did not realize that a lack of audience participation diminishes the retention and usefulness of what is taught.

Joe should have written discussion questions and directed the trainers to organize small groups. He should have included ways for everyone to try out the equipment and to practice the techniques for breathing and keeping calm. He could have written role-plays or games. Because he simulated a disaster, he could also have written a simulation for the participants to role play. There also should have been some kind of on-the-job follow-up such as assignments requiring participants to locate escape routes, to locate and shut off gas valves, and to amass emergency supplies.

Obviously, participation is key to retention and application of learning. Some creative trainers can think of learning activities on their feet. Most trainers, however, are too busy keeping track of the program to simultaneously create activities; therefore, learning activities must be designed in advance. This chapter tell how to succeed at creating inventive, original learning activities.

Books like the *Handbooks of Structured Experiences for Human Relations Training* (Pfeiffer & Jones, 1969-1985) contain ready-to-use learning activities. Designers can use them as they appear in the books or create new activities for the particular training program.

WRITING DISCUSSIONS

Active and participating audiences learn and remember more than passive audiences. Discussions involve audiences by eliciting responses, and discussion questions are among the easiest kinds of learning activities to write. When people talk about a concept or skill, they become more involved with it because they have invested some of themselves and their energy into it. Below are some sample discussion questions designed to involve the participants after the trainer has introduced the objectives. These are open-ended questions that do not allow a simple yes-or-no answer but require the participant to share what he or she thinks.

- How does this relate to what you wanted?
- How does this interest you?
- How does this satisfy your needs?
- What more do you want?
- How would you like to add to or change this?

A good trainer has to be skilled in leading discussions. Because each group of learners is different, the trainer will ask many spontaneous questions, but the training designer can keep the program on track by writing questions and suggested responses. Prepared questions lead the participants to discover ideas or ways of doing things, to reinforce what the trainer presented, and to apply what they have learned.

Discovering Questions

The previous chapter discussed ways of writing explanations. However, explanations do not always have to be handed out to the participants. Rather, the training designer can also think of questions that lead participants to discover answers. If possible, the designer can phrase the questions in such a way as to utilize the more experienced participants' expertise. This will publicly acknowledge those participants' expertise and will appeal to their sense of professional pride. Designers should provide exact wording for the questions rather than stating, "The trainer should ask about..."

The training designer can help the facilitator guide the audience to a conclusion through a series of questions. This approach is based on the concept called *inductive reasoning*. Inductive reasoning is the Socratic approach to problem solving that is based on the Platonic belief that we already know these answers but are just not aware of them. Figure 5-2 provides a series of sample discovery questions.

This example might seem simplistic and yet, if a number of supervisors were verbally abusing employees, this knowledge could be new to them. This style of questioning leads the participants to volunteer the answers themselves, which has more impact on the participants than if an outside "authority" were to tell it to them. Saying something oneself reinforces one's acceptance and belief of the idea or concept being stated.

Questions require the participants to make use of one of two main types of reasoning to reach their conclusions: *inductive reasoning* or *deductive reasoning*. Inductive reasoning is based on a series of facts or observations, from which is drawn a general conclusion. The training designer can supply facts and observations through demonstrations, role plays, videos, or questions alone. Short reading passages could also be used.

Trainer: Let's say I'm a supervisor.

Directions: Walk up to one person in the audience and pretend that he or she is your employee.

Trainer (in loud, angry voice): I was just here to help you with the telephone and now you want help with the computer. Why didn't you ask me before? I can't keep running back and forth.

Trainer (addressing audience in normal voice): What did you observe?

Probable Answer: Supervisor yelling at employee.

Trainer: How do you think the employee felt?

Probable Answer: Hurt

Trainer: What do you think that did to the employee's motivation and productivity?

Probable Answer: Lowered them.

Trainer: What can we conclude?

Probable Answer: Yelling lowers motivation.

Trainer: If we want motivated, productive employees, what should we do?

Probable Answer: Speak to them kindly.

Figure 5-2. Sample Discovery Questions

Deductive reasoning moves from the general to the specific. The training designer can direct the trainer to work the audience through to a conclusion from a general statement in order to discover more information about it. Figure 5-3 illustrates deductive reasoning.

Trainer: Employees are happier and more productive when they have the power to make some decisions about their working conditions. When would employee decision making work best here?

Possible answers: When making changes; when implementing new programs.

Trainer: What are some things we could do?

Possible answers: Utilize quality circles; solicit employee suggestions.

Figure 5-3. Illustration of Deductive Reasoning

Deductive reasoning is most effective when the participants already understand and accept a general concept but are not sure of the details or may not understand how the abstract concept applies to their situation. The questioning process involved in deductive reasoning helps them to recognize and understand the details. Used in this fashion, the deductive process works in a manner similar to the way that analogies and allegories were discussed in the last chapter. With analogies and allegories, the trainer states a new piece of information and tells a story that is familiar to the participants. However, with deductive reasoning, the trainer does not make the connection; rather, the designer writes a series of questions that leads the participants to make the connection. Figure 5-4 provides further examples of deductive questions.

Teaching with questions as a method of encouraging participants to discover new information works best when the skills and concepts that are being taught are already somewhat familiar. If the participants are new to the organization, unfamiliar with the subject matter, if new technology is being introduced, or if the material is so complex that a skilled facilitator must explain it, the training designer will have to reserve trainers' questions for other portions of the program. Moreover, the trainer's questions should not require participants to guess what the trainer is thinking, but rather should reinforce what the participants have learned.

Trainer: A computer is similar to a typewriter. Which keys do both have in common?

Possible answers: Letters, numbers, space bar, backspace key.

Trainer: What on a typewriter is equivalent to the computer screen?

Answer: Paper.

Trainer: What would the cursor on a computer keyboard correspond to on a typewriter?

Answer: Location of the carriage.

Figure 5-4. Sample Deductive Questions

Writing Reinforcing Questions

After an explanation, possibly in conjunction with a video or with some of the techniques suggested in Chapter 4, the next step often is to have the trainer question the participants. This gives the participants an opportunity to put their newfound knowledge to work and tests their learning. The trainer should not ask, "What did I just say?" Therefore, the designer should create specific questions. To ensure that the participants feel comfortable with the questions, the designer can help the trainer to start with questions that have no right or wrong answers and to ask for opinions—such as those listed in Figure 5-5.

- What do you think of this?

- How could this help on your job?

- Why do you like this way of doing it?

- How do you feel about it?

Figure 5-5. Sample Open-Ended Questions

Participants can often be encouraged to participate in the discussion if they are asked to respond to questions that offer them choices. For example: "Would you talk to the customer or the employee first? Why?"

The designer can choose to have the trainer drill the participants with a battery of questions. The trainer can use flash cards to teach people to recognize terms, symbols, certain kinds of identification cards, and so on. The trainer may have to ask questions again and again until he or she is certain that all the participants understand. This can be an effective technique when it is essential that the learners recognize or memorize something.

To review and summarize the program, have the trainer ask about each part. At this point, trainers can ask specific factual questions. For example:

- How do you start?
- What is (skill or concept)?
- Why is it important?
- What will you remember about (skill or concept)?

Writing Questions that Apply the Skill

Discovery and review questions usually elicit only a few answers from a group. However, the training designer can create opportunities for discussions that stimulate more participation. These types of discussions will be closer to more complex learning activities. To prepare for an "applying" discussion, the designer must write not only questions for the trainer but also directions for organizing the group. Brainstorming, debates, and small-group discussions are examples of applying discussions.

Brainstorming gives the participants the opportunity to generate a series of options without fear of censorship or derision. Brainstorming is an effective way of getting creative, new ideas. The rules of brainstorming are to list as many ideas as possible, even unusual or "off-the-wall" ones, and not to judge or eliminate them until a later time. It can be used to generate a list of examples, of uses of a skill, or of solutions to a problem. If ideas, energy, or creativity in the group begins to lag, the trainer can switch the topic of the brainstorming, perhaps to a silly topic. This way, the tension to produce ideas is alleviated and participants relax and will most likely think of new ideas when they are steered back to the original topic. Figure 5-6 provides a sample script for a brainstorming session.

Another way to get participants talking more about something is to stage a debate. First, debates do not need to mimic formalized forensics teams. The group can be split in half, with one side directed to be "pro" and the other to be "con." One side could be asked to express employees' views and the other side to express management's views. The trainer then asks both sides questions. Each side can address the other side's answers. Figure 5-7 provides a sample script for a debate.

If a team consists of more than ten people, chances are that not everyone will participate. People tend to feel more comfortable and therefore to speak more when in small groups. On the other hand, a group split into several teams misses the trainer's leadership and the opportunity to observe

Trainer: Let's list all the examples of positive feedback to an employee. Remember, any idea goes here. Nothing's too trivial or obvious to exclude. Everyone will contribute an idea.

Directions: List ideas on flip chart. Call on people until the group seems to have run out of new ideas.

Trainer: Now, let's brainstorm about another topic for a moment. I want you to think of what you would like in your ideal car if you were the designer.

Directions: List car ideas.

Trainer: Now, let's get back to our original topic: positive feedback for employees. What other examples do you have of positive feedback?

Figure 5-6. Sample Script for a Brainstorming Session

the interaction of the other teams. Setting up each team with detailed directions or appointing team leaders can help make up for the lack of skilled direction, and asking each team to prepare a group report can serve as a forum for total-group sharing. Obviously, the training designer needs to write instructions for how the trainer should organize the teams, how the trainer should give instructions, and what questions the trainer should ask the teams.

The designer can choose to have each team discuss the same questions or to have each team discuss a different issue. Teams can be organized according to where people are sitting, by their individual areas of specialty, or by having people count off. The counting method is good for mixing up groups who have already worked together or who already know one another. Figure 5-8 provides a sample script for small-group discussions.

When very large groups are broken into smaller groups, one small group can discuss while the others listen. This group-within-a-group method is sometimes referred to as a"fishbowl" design. Remember that, if the purpose of the group-within-group setup is to reinforce or apply ideas, only those in the small group get first-hand experience. On the other hand, the group within a group can be used to hone observation skills or to teach analysis of group dynamics or meetings.

One group-within-group setup that is effective for teaching people how groups operate is the *leaderless group*. The leaderless group can help in discovering ideas about leadership. It also can help answer the following questions about leadership and group dynamics: How does it feel to be the leader? The follower? The talker? The passive participant? Who talks to whom?

Directions: Ask participants to stand or move chairs to split the group into two equal-sized groups.

Trainer: We're going to have a debate about rural versus urban health care. This side (pointing) will be rural and this side (pointing) will be urban. Take a few minutes to think about what you've already learned.

Now, starting with the rural side, what's one advantage to being a patient living in a rural area?

What does the urban side have to say about that suggestion?

Urban side, what's one advantage of being a patient who lives in the city?

What does the rural side say to that suggestion?

Directions: Continue to ask the same questions to get three to four advantages for each side. Ask the groups to debate aspects such as hospital specialization, access to hospitals, presence or absence of family support systems, personalized attention, and access to specialized equipment.

Figure 5-7. Sample Script for Debate

The method of selection used to determine which trainees will be active participants in the group-within-group setup can be determined by either the designer or the trainer. Participants may be chosen by random selection, by occupational specialty or another factor, or on a volunteer basis. It is best for the training designer to choose a topic for discussion that involves controversy so those participating will respond actively to different sides of an issue. The designer must specify what the small group is to do, what the large group is to do, and how the trainer should guide them. Figure 5-9 presents a sample script for leaderless-group facilitation.

Directions: Organize the group into three small groups based on which section people are most familiar with: hardware, appliances, or gifts.

Trainer: We're going to work in groups to find ways to cut costs in your department. You will be given fifteen minutes to discuss this problem. Then each group will share its ideas.

Directions: Allow fifteen minutes. Visit each group to make sure that it is on target and to listen for ideas.

Trainer (after 15 minutes): What are some ideas that the hardware group had? Can the rest of you add to that?

Directions: Continue with each group. Try to get more than one group member involved each time that a group participates.

Figure 5-8. Sample Script for Small-Group Discussions

Whether the design calls for small-group interaction or a group-within-group activity, some sort of reporting-out activity that allows the groups to summarize their accomplishments and to share their learnings will need to follow.

This follow-up activity can be designed in various ways. Each group could create a report, perhaps by summarizing on flip charts, or each group could report orally to the rest of the participants. The desired method should be specified in the training design. If a group spokesperson is needed, either the group or the trainer may choose him or her. In addition, be sure to specify in the design how the trainer should organize the groups' reports.

Preparatory note to trainer: Note which participants are most articulate.

Directions: Choose six of the most articulate participants and ask them to sit around a circular table that is either in the front of the room or in the center of the room; this will make it easy for the other participants to turn and observe.

Trainer: The people at this table are going to read the directions on their handouts; then, they will discuss the following topic: Whether the city should put in a park or a parking lot on a site in their neighborhood. I will stop the group after twenty minutes, and one of you should write the group's decision on this flip chart. The rest of you have received a checklist; please use it to record your observations. Now read your handouts and begin discussing.

Directions: Do not say anything to get the participants started or to help them. Stop the discussion after twenty minutes.

Figure 5-9. Sample Script for Leaderless-Group Facilitation

If the group is too large or if there is not enough time for the small-group work and reporting, the designer can substitute a series of discussion questions or a short poll in which the entire group can participate.

DESIGNING COMPLEX LEARNING ACTIVITIES

Some training requires participation in complicated hands-on activities. This sometimes is necessary in order for trainees to gain confidence in difficult skills, to experiment with and learn potentially dangerous procedures, or to give them the opportunity to figure out skills on their own and to answer their own questions. Examples of complex learning activities include role plays, case studies, field trips, games, and using products or equipment. Some activities provide more hypothetical experience; others come very close to on-the-job training.

Role Plays

For training in management skills or any kind of interpersonal skills such as communication, customer relations, sales, or supervising, role plays allow learners to "try out" the skills in the most direct and realistic way. Role plays can also be used to help learners discover theories and principles for themselves.

The only drawback of role playing is that participants often feel awkward about "playacting" and are shy about getting up in front of the group. Thus, people often are slow to volunteer to take part in a role play. Trainers can call on one or two participants to role play, which can embarrass the selected persons and can also prevent others from trying out the skills. Therefore, it is best to let everyone role play simultaneously. Be sure to include some kind of reassurance in the trainer's directions, such as "This may not feel natural" or "Role playing is like an athlete exercising one muscle group to prepare for the game." Another analogy frequently used is that role playing is like learning to drive in the parking lot before venturing onto the highway.

Role plays in groups of one to four work best. Designers can set up the activity so that individuals role play or respond according to a handout, which will be discussed in further detail in Chapter 6. The trainer can play a role (a difficult employee, a customer, or a vendor, for example) and interact with several different people in order to make them respond and to use certain skills. Similarly, each participant could respond to an audiotaped situation. Some learning labs—such as the ones used in foreign-language classes—provide the opportunity to respond in a role-play fashion.

Role plays also can be enacted without the trainer's participation. This technique is faster and gets everyone involved. When groups of three and four work together, one or more people can serve as observers or coaches, thus providing an alternative way of putting the desired skills to use. Extra people can also be incorporated into the role play through the addition of "supporting" roles such as a second disgruntled customer or another striking union worker. Keep in mind, however, that three roles is usually the maximum for a successful role play, although a creative designer could have the trainer assign each person in a group a role to simulate an entire organization. Remember that the more people in a role play, the longer it takes, particularly if each person has ample opportunity to participate and test new skills.

Write detailed instructions for what the trainer should say and do during the administration of the role play. A written situation for the role play for the trainees is also helpful. The trainer should demonstrate how a role play works, modeling the desired behavior so that participants are more sure of what to do. When giving directions, the trainer should tell the participants the purpose of the role play, the logistics of getting organized, and exactly what each participant will be doing, including time restraints. Figure 5-10 provides a sample script for role-play facilitation.

Role plays need a conclusion—a reminder to the participants of why they took part and what they accomplished. The conclusion can take the form of an oral report from each

Trainer: We're going to practice the delegation skills that we have been discussing. I'm going to organize you into groups of three. One person will be the manager, one will play the role of an employee, and the third will be an observer who will help the manager delegate properly. I'll be giving you each an assignment to delegate. The manager will follow the steps. The employee will ask questions if the directions are not clear and will answer any questions that the manager asks. Don't worry about what to say; what you say is less important than the process by which you do things. Just make up something if you are asked a question. The observer will use the checklist to record examples of the manager's delegation skills. Each manager will have five minutes to prepare and five minutes to delegate. Observers will have five minutes to give feedback. After that, you'll switch roles and I'll give you a different handout. Remember that the reason for doing this is to try out the delegation skills that you've learned and to become more comfortable using them.

First, I'll show you how it's going to work. I'm going to delegate the task of reorganizing the files to (name of participant). All of you should check on me to see if I do it right.

Trainer (to participant)**:** I'd like you to reorganize the files. I want all the records older than 1980 to be thrown out. Then I'd like you to put them in alphabetical order by the name of the company rather than by the date so we can locate them more easily. How do you think you'll do this? Can you finish by Wednesday? I'll check back later today to see if you need any help.

Trainer (to group)**:** How did I do? How thoroughly did I cover each step? What I did is what the manager will do, and what you did is what the observer will do.

Directions: Point to each person, giving him or her a role. Choose groups to role play. Distribute appropriate handouts to each role player. Walk around and monitor the groups as they role play. Notify them when time is up; choose another person to play the role of manager.

Figure 5-10. Sample Script for Role-Play Facilitation

group; of a general discussion; or of the trainer's comments and observations about how the groups operated.

Case Studies

Case studies are in some ways similar to small-group discussions and role plays, but they also can be structured as individual activities. In a case study, groups or individuals respond to a description of a specific situation; but unlike a role play, the respondents do not have to play the part of someone else. Case studies can achieve the same goals as role plays; they also can go beyond one-on-one interaction to consider broader issues, such as strategic planning.

Case studies can be written material (created perhaps by the designer), videotaped situations, or articles from outside sources. Participants apply their new-found skills by analyzing the case study, which can take the form of a group discussion if desired. The group may be assigned one or more of the following tasks: (1) to decide what the problem is, (2) to find a solution, (3) to find errors or mistakes in the case, or (4) to indicate how to do a procedure correctly.

Davies (1981) lists four types of case studies:

1. *Critical incidents* require participants to analyze a mistake or conflict to determine what further information they need, what probably caused the problem, and what should happen next.

2. *Stage cases* require participants to read about stages that preceded an event and to decide what should happen next.

3. *Live cases* involve a crisis or situation that takes place *during* the training, such as a major news event. Participants discuss the event and follow the news to find out how the crisis unfolds and how it is resolved.

4. *Major issue cases* involve a problem that is buried in contradictory data. The object is to sort out what information is important, what is extraneous, and what the real problem is.

Research and observation often turn up situations for case studies, examples of misuses, or outstanding use of certain skills. Case studies can be about people, facts, or figures. Figure 5-11 provides a sample script for case-study administration.

Trainer: I'm going to give you a case study to read, and you'll also see some questions with it. Read the case to decide where and how you would begin to figure out the cause of this problem.

Directions: Hand out cases. Allow the participants thirty minutes to complete instructions.

Trainer: What did you decide?

Directions: Post responses on flip chart.

Figure 5-11. Sample Script for Case-Study Administration

The participants should have a discussion after they work through a case, so the training designer should write some discussion questions. Sometimes case studies will spur the participants to write a report or to develop a plan. This affords an excellent opportunity for skills practice.

Field Trips

The designer may choose to have the trainer take the trainees out of the classroom. Field trips allow participants to observe processes that in turn become in-class activities and mini-case studies. The trainer can take participants to actual work places to learn about team effectiveness, employee relations, or customer service, for example. Here, the participants apply what they learned by looking for it. Afterward, the trainer can lead a group discussion, or the participants can write down their suggestions for changing the situation.

A field trip also is a good exercise in observation skills or note taking. Some places may provide one-way mirrors for unobtrusive group observation, such as at a child-care facility, a hospital (to observe patient-doctor interaction), or at a focus group.

The training designer should either secure permission for these visits or should direct the trainer or participants to make the arrangements. If the trip occurs within the context of a seminar, this should be indicated. The designer should set the observation requirements and create accompanying classroom activities.

The example in Figure 5-12 illustrates how a field trip can complement a training session on how to set up training rooms. Since a picture may be worth a thousand words, a field trip to various training locations enables trainees to see various setups and to observe them being used. The trainer may suggest that the trainees critique each site visited or that they incorporate their favorite aspects of each site to produce a diagram of their ideal training-room arrangement.

Games

Some training situations require trainees to learn many facts, to memorize procedures, or to answer a long series of questions. Training games offer fun and a creative alternative for practice and memorization. Designers and trainers need to realize, however, that some groups might feel too inhibited to play games.

The organization of games is a creative part of the design process. Designers can get ideas from popular board games or from television game shows. They also can design games that are modeled on contests (e.g., count the number of jelly beans in the jar; name a slogan; or eat the most pie). Board games and quiz shows can be used to drill participants on skills or concepts, while contests can test speed, dexterity, or accuracy.

Handout: Checklist for Training-Room Arrangements

Trainer: We're going to visit four sites this week, so you can look for the principles of training-room arrangement that we've discussed. Please feel free to ask questions as we go along. This checklist will guide you in looking for all the items that we've mentioned. Make sure you check something at every site. Then, when we meet here again, your assignment will be to redesign one of the rooms that we visit or to suggest a brand-new design.

Figure 5-12. Sample Script for Field-Trip Instructions

Board games work best with small groups of two to six participants. Create a board with a path or grid drawn on it and include some way for participants to move their pawns along the path, such as with dice or cards. The path or boxes can ask questions or direct participants to draw cards that test their skills and knowledge.

The designer needs to write the text of the board, the cards (if used), and the game directions. The designer or a graphic artist may create the board itself. On a more individualized basis, the designer can create crossword puzzles that let the participants work with the jargon of a job or skill.

With bigger groups, or if the designer simply is looking for a different kind of activity, consider staging a quiz show. The team atmosphere of quiz shows taps people's competitive nature. The facilitator acts as the master of ceremonies (MC). Two or more teams challenge one another. The designer writes the MC's questions and sets up the quiz show. The participants may choose categories, bid on points for questions, try to answer questions first, and so on. Determine a way to keep score and decide what the winning score will be.

Figure 5-13 provides an example of a game for a training program on the legalities of employee relations. For this quiz show, there are questions on various topics, and the participants are divided into competing teams.

A contest can be set up as a type of role play or as a hands-on test of speed or accuracy. In an example of another type of contest, teams could test their keypunching accuracy in timed sessions to see which team enters the most data with the fewest errors. As with all types of games, the

---

Trainer: We're going to play a game to give you an opportunity to apply what you've learned about legal questions about employee rights. We'll form three teams of eight persons each. First, two teams will play against each other and the third team will challenge the winner. Your teams will take turns sending one person up to answer a question, relay style. Questions will be in the following categories: hiring, sexual harassment, discipline, and termination. There will be question cards for each category and a flip chart for scorekeeping. A participant will choose the category and, if he or she cannot answer the question, the other team will be given an opportunity to try. After each player has had a turn, the team with the most points will be the winner.

Directions: Divide participants into teams. Line up two teams opposite each other. Call on one player at a time; ask him or her to choose a category; then ask the player a question. Keep score on a flip chart. Restate the learning objectives of the game.

Trainer: This game has given you practice in answering various employer questions about the law and employee rights. You all answered well, so now you'll have some answers and you will know how to find others when you're on the job.

Figure 5-13. Sample Script for Quiz-Show Facilitation

designer should give the trainer a description and tell him or her how to assign roles, how the contest should begin and end, and how to explain the purpose of the game.

CREATING REALISTIC TRAINING SESSIONS

Design training situations that are as realistic as possible. Incorporate the necessary products and equipment, and stage the activity in a true-to-life setting. Realize that most people learn best through hands-on experience; for example, salespeople need product knowledge, which is best gained by having them use the products. Similarly, people cannot learn to use machines, tools, vehicles, and so on, unless they try them out. One way to do this is simply to tell the participants to use the item—to try it out and to experiment with it. Make it possible for each learner to practice the skills and to receive some performance feedback. This helps participants to feel more confident about using the skills, which results in a higher likelihood that they will use the skills correctly on the job. It also lets the trainer know whether to go on or to allow the participants more practice time.

Another, better method is to set up laboratory situations that structure the participants' learning. This ensures consistency and eases the trainers' position. In this case, the role of the designer is to indicate what equipment is needed, how the participants should be organized, and what work sheets (such as checklists or instruction sheets) should be distributed.

Of course, the bigger and bulkier the equipment or tools, the more difficult it is to bring them into a classroom. Trainers often must use simulators or parts of items under these circumstances. For example, an automobile-repair session may use an engine rather than an entire car. Commercial airlines and the armed forces do much of their pilot training on simulators rather than in jets. Creative thinking will suggest ways to give learners hands-on experience even without "the real thing."

Each hands-on activity should include feedback and follow-up steps so that participants know how they did and where they should go with their learning. If the group might be too large for the trainer to give individual feedback, the designer should include an alternate method of feedback. For example, dyads could give each other feedback, other outside experts could comment, or the trainer could ask the early finishers to observe and comment on the other learners.

Of course, not all skills and training involve machines, tools, or manual skills exclusively. Many tasks and skills also involve mental skills such as writing—letters, memos, forms, notations, reports, or proposals, for example. Many helpful writing activities can be incorporated into training sessions. The designer can have the participants study a case study or video and then ask them to write a related letter or fill out a related form. For example, police-department trainees could watch a video of an automobile break-in and then be told to fill out the arrest form. In this case, the training designer should list the forms needed, explain how the facilitator should set up the activity, and write the scenario. Training people to write reports or to fill out forms may need to include some information about research. In this case, the trainer needs to have on hand any reference guides, lists, etc., that are used in the particular work environment. Trainees should become familiar with these references, perhaps through activities in which they have to use the references to complete forms.

Other types of skills require writing as well. For example, many training sessions are conducted on time management, organization, delegation, and planning. An effective learning tool for all of these types of sessions is the *in-basket activity*. In an in-basket activity, the designer generates a number of possible items of correspondence that a person in that organization or position could receive: letters, memos, junk mail, reports, items needing approval, and telephone messages. The object is for the trainee to go through his or her "in-basket," prioritizing, delegating, handling, or discarding as needed. The training designer needs to write out the trainer's role, instructions for the trainees, and the goals of the activity (see Figure 5-14).

Trainer: To give you practice on categorizing and prioritizing, as we've discussed, you'll each be going through a typical package of memos, requests, reports, and other paperwork that a supervisor might find in his or her in-basket. Go through everything, prioritize each item, and write down your reasons for your decisions. Remember that not everything in your in-basket needs to be handled by you personally—or even needs to be handled at all. You have thirty minutes to complete this activity; then we'll see what you came up with.

Figure 5-14. Sample Script for In-Basket Activity

CHAPTER SUMMARY

This chapter has described many detailed ways to create learning activities that tell trainers what to do and say. The designer has a variety of options for creating discussions, role plays, case studies, games, and hands-on experiences. Most of these activities require supplemental materials such as handouts, work sheets, manuals, checklists, and instructions, all of which must be created in advance by the training designer.

As we move through the training design, we can see that the points covered form a sort of design or leaders' guide containing the following components:

1. Objective of the learning activity
2. Materials or handouts for the learning activity
3. Type of learning activity
   - Role plays
   - Case studies
   - Field trips
   - Games
   - Hands-on experience with products or equipment

4. Directions and dialog for the trainer
5. Follow-up and feedback upon completion of the learning activity.

REFERENCES

Davies, I.K. (1981). *Instructional technique.* New York: McGraw-Hill.

Pfeiffer, J.W., & Jones, J.E. (Eds.). (1969-1985). *A handbook of structured experiences for human relations training* (Vols. I through X). San Diego, CA: University Associates.

6

WRITING HANDOUTS AND TRAINING MANUALS

Leslie developed a training program for secretaries. Through the needs assessment that she conducted in the organization, she discovered that most secretaries already knew how to type, and they also tested well on the use of phones and filing systems. What they needed most was to learn more about the company's word-processing system, *Word.* The secretaries were using the word processor as if it were a typewriter; they were unaware of its more sophisticated functions.

Leslie planned the training session to include a general review of computers, followed by an outline of the uses and functions of word processing. As developmental resources, she planned to use both the application manuals and those people who had used the applications. Leslie planned four half-day sessions with one week between each session to give the learners the opportunity for on-the-job practice. Figure 6-1 shows Leslie's program outline.

Leslie designed an interesting introduction that included a demonstration of how much time and effort word processors save. She mentioned how much time the secretaries would save when they no longer had to retype paragraphs or to create new letters for every person. Then she wrote an overview of what computers could do for them, and she wrote instructions for the trainer.

Leslie wrote easy-to-understand definitions of each step for the trainer to give as answers. She had a graphic designer create colorful posters illustrating the functions of various command keys. Her boss allowed her to purchase a projector that could show what was on the word processing screen so that the trainer could demonstrate on a large scale. Leslie's examples were very relevant to the word-processing functions that the secretaries wanted to learn; and she used many analogies comparing such things as computer files to filing cabinets. Her transitions were smooth, relating each part of the session to the next.

Training Objective: Secretaries will use more sophisticated features of Word, including the following:

Move and Copy

Columns

Spell-Check and Thesaurus

Merge Lists

Figure 6-1. Leslie's Program Outline

Each explanation was followed by questions to review the points covered and to make sure that the secretaries understood them. In a small-group discussion, the trainer would ask participants to discuss the uses and applications of the merge function.

The main part of the program consisted of hands-on activities in a training room with terminals. The trainees spent most of the sessions practicing on the computers. Leslie wrote instructions and scripts dictating what the trainer should do and say. She also worked in some spelling-bee games in which the trainees practiced retrieving definitions. A contest determined who could input the most data with the fewest errors. The winner would receive a small plaque that attached to a terminal and read, "I'm the best!"

In an elaborate concluding activity, the trainees watched a video of a supervisor requesting information and a report from a secretary. The supervisor told the secretaries what to input into their computers; they then asked the group to generate the report and explain the word-processing steps to a partner. Leslie also included excellent summaries for each module that asked the trainees to repeat the main points and that encouraged them to use the word processor and its features.

What was Leslie's mistake? She created no handouts—nothing to guide participants through the seminar, nothing to help them remember what they had learned back on the job. The only thing she had written for the participants was the preassignment. In a memo announcing the seminar, she wrote: "Please look over the Word manual." Unfortunately, the Word manual was lengthy and difficult to understand. Most of the secretaries gave up trying to understand paragraphs such as:

> When automatic hyphenation is chosen, words will be automatically hyphenated by a set of functions within Word. Words with two or more syllables will disunite at the appropriate division unless a menu appears on the screen or unless the proper noun character has been defaulted. To deactivate the automatic hyphenation, proceed through the macro codes to the wrap option and select the appropriate preference.

Many secretaries misunderstood the preassignment. One looked only at the cover of the manual; some skimmed the manual; the few that tried to read it were unable to understand it. The trainees needed more specific instructions and a preassignment that made sense.

When trainers conducted the program, the trainees asked so many questions that some trainers ran out of time and were unable to cover some of the crucial points. Because of the absence of an agenda, trainees occasionally became confused by trainers' explanations and had to ask for clarification as to how various points fit into the larger picture.

When the trainees were divided into discussion groups, no written instructions or questions were provided to guide them. Again, they asked, "What are we supposed to do? Who does what?" The spelling bee had no instructions or written objectives. A checklist for each topic could have helped them to see the point of what they learned.

Even though the trainers gave good directions for the hands-on activities, the trainees lost track of what to input and the proper sequence for data entry.

While videos were good substitutes for case studies, the participants still needed something to refer to when they had additional work to do with a case. The role plays also should have included instructions.

When they went back to work and tried to utilize the advanced Word functions, the secretaries forgot even some of the simpler definitions and functions. They were forced to telephone the trainers and ask for explanations. They had taken no notes, and they had no easy way to look up what they had practiced in the training sessions.

The secretaries had a strong need to use what they learned. A how-to reference—perhaps a card attached to their computer monitors—would have helped.

Varied activities stimulate learning, while applied activities increase learners' chances of remembering and using skills back on the job. Activities enhance explanations, and written note-taking guides, questions, and instructions facilitate effective discussions and hands-on activities. Finally, the spoken word is easily forgotten, but putting something in writing allows visual learning and is permanent enough to be a reference.

Handouts, work sheets, training manuals, overheads, flip charts, and job aids guide participants through workshops, focusing them on the subject and making it easier for them to follow the training. In addition, written materials that learners can take away serve as reference guides that can help train others.

Handouts differ from flip charts and overheads in that the writing can be more detailed—more like text than notes or highlights. Overhead projections and flip charts must be read from a distance, so the text itself should be large and uncluttered; a projection or reproduction of a typewritten page is too difficult for an audience to read. A few words and phrases should be written on each overhead transparency or flip chart; complete sentences or more than five to seven lines are usually too much. Flip charts are handy for posting, while overhead projections can be seen by a larger audience. In lieu of notes, many trainers use overheads to guide participants through presentations. Later, participants may receive handouts identical to the overhead transparencies for reference.

As a writer, the job of the training designer is to use a language and style that enables the trainer to communicate most effectively with the participants. Unlike other types of training-related writing, such as the writing of the training map or the detailed training design, handouts are for the trainees, not the trainers. Therefore, straightforward, simple language with short questions and sentences works best. The layout of the handout and possibly the use of figures or tables on handouts also affect the handout's readability, but we will not cover layout and design here.

Written materials for distribution to participants complement each of the training methods discussed in previous chapters. Handouts can aid explanations by guiding note taking, by listing topics, or by giving an overview of discussions and steps. Discussions also run more smoothly when participants can read either the questions or the objectives of the discussion. Most learning activities require the use of written materials for maximum effectiveness.

WRITING FOR PARTICIPANT USE

Training designers can create five kinds of writing with the participants in mind: (1) directions for learning activities, (2) questions for handouts, (3) fill-in-the-blank sentences, (4) headlines, which subtitle handouts, facilitate note taking and observation, and are used to make up job guides, and (5) scenarios, which narrate case studies and certain role plays. Table 6-1 depicts the five types of participant-focused training writing and the kinds of activities for which they are used.

Table 1. Types of Writing for Trainees

	Note Taking	Over Heads or Flip Charts	Discus-sion Groups	Case Studies	Field Trips	Games	Role Plays / Hands On	Job Guides
Directions		X	X	X	X	X	X	
Questions	X	X	X	X	X	X	X	
Fill In the Blanks	X				X		X	
Headlines	X	X			X		X	X
Scenarios			X	X				

Directions

Almost all learning activities, including preassignments, can be made more understandable to participants with well-written directions. Written directions should be as specific and detailed as possible. However, learners should not have to wade through several pages before discovering what they are supposed to do. Make directions as concise and brief as possible without leaving anything out. Consider the following questions.

- For a preassignment, which pages should the participants read, and how carefully should they read them? Will the participants be tested on what they read? What will they do with what they read?
- If the preassignment is to conduct an interview, who should be interviewed? How many questions should the interviewers ask? How long should the interview take?

- If the participants are given a preassignment to bring something to the training session, where can they find it and what is it? How long will it take to find the object?
- If the participants are asked to observe something, what, where, when, and how should it be observed? How will they prove that they completed the assignment? What will they do with the knowledge at the session?

The above questions also apply to field-trip observations that trainers conduct in conjunction with training sessions.

Similarly, designers should write directions for any group discussions, case studies, games, or role plays that will be conducted during the training session. The word-processing training session that Leslie designed should have included directions for the group discussion, the spelling bee, the hands-on computer practice, the video-based role play.

Training developers should write directions in the *imperative* or *command* verb form, which is the simplest, most straightforward way to direct someone to action. Add "please" to be polite. For example, "Now, please turn to your partner and tell him or her your impressions of the video." The participants will appreciate a sentence or two about the purpose or goal of the directions. Supply details such as how long the participants should spend on each instruction. List the steps in the order that they should occur.

Directions pertaining to discussion groups will usually be instructions to answer certain questions. Consider the following when creating instructions: Should the group choose a leader? Should someone take notes? Will the group report or summarize the discussion?

Case-study directions should guide participants' reading and tell them what they should do as a result of their reading. For example, the directions might say, "Read the following case study to discover what the problem is. Then write the problem in the form of an open-ended question. You will have twenty minutes to do this task."

Instructions for a game should not be as complicated as the long and detailed rule books found in conventional games. Simply state the rules of the game. What does each player do? Do they roll dice or draw a card? How do they proceed? How does a player win? If the game is like a game show, the directions should specify the number of contestants, the method of regulating the contestants' play, how many points questions are worth, and what constitutes elimination. The writing on cards or squares may also be directions. Write brief commands and conditional (if/then) statements. For example, "Answer the question correctly and take another turn. If you answer incorrectly, you must go back to square one."

Directions for role plays also state rules and conditions. How many players? What is each player's role? How long should the role play last? What should the players do and why? There often will be a different instruction page for each participant in a role play. If the participants are unfamiliar with role playing, the designer can help them by writing their opening lines. For example, the participant may begin by saying, "I'd like to help you improve." However, do not supply a complete role-play script; this defeats the purpose of the activity.

While role-play instructions differ for each role or position, participants in hands-on activities usually do the same thing. The designer needs to specify how the activities will proceed: in pairs, groups, or individually. What equipment should the participants use? Is there a time limit? List the desired actions in steps. When writing a training manual for on-the-job practice, include not only detailed instructions but names of resources, phone numbers of people to call for help, and instructions for processing completed exercises.

Questions

Training designers write questions for needs assessments and for discussion scripts. The open-ended question is common. Designers also must learn to write handout questions that parallel the trainer's questions.

Clever placement of open-ended questions can facilitate participants' note taking. For example, the handout may ask the participants to record their own definitions or examples. This method of writing handouts especially complements discussions, but it also works when the trainer first gives an explanation and then asks the learners to restate the explanation in their own words. This helps participants to understand what the trainer has said and increases the chances that they will remember what they have learned. Similarly, writing questions can guide the learners to the most important points of an upcoming video, presentation, or activity. For example, the participants could be provided with a list of questions that they will be able to answer after watching a videotape, such as "What is cholesterol? Why are the X valves important? What is the first step in starting WORD?"

The design of a small-group discussion should include the questions that the group should be discussing. The designer also can write instructions and suggest time limits. The design for a small-group discussion can include not only open-ended questions but a brainstorming or free-writing activity (such as making a list) to generate ideas.

The design of a case study or a field trip could include questions that show learners how to gain from their experience. Answering the questions then becomes a discussion-group or individual activity.

The designer can create game questions for the trainer to write on a board or on cards. The key to writing these questions is to make sure they have one clear and indisputable answer. Game questions should not be like discussion questions, which have no one correct answer. In this respect, game questions are similar to fill-in-the-blank statements.

Fill-in-the-Blank Statements

Some note-taking guides feature fill-in-the-blank sentences. As the trainer talks, the participants fill in the blanks. While this can be helpful in that it alerts participants about important points, it can also be a distraction. Some participants may become more concerned with listening for the key words in order to complete the blanks than with trying to understand what the speaker is saying. Filling in the blanks can work if the sentences with blanks do not follow one another too closely in a presentation. Because the blanks draw attention to the words that occupy them, they are most effective in training situations in which it is most important for trainees to remember terms or names. Fill-in-the-blank activities achieve the opposite goal than do discussion questions. Fill-in-the-blanks encourage learners to remember key words or short phrases; discussion questions encourage learners to remember definitions and examples.

Fill-in-the-blanks are occasionally appropriate for use in conjunction with field trips or hands-on experience. For example, cosmetology students could experiment with hair-color products or observe a beauty-school demonstration. For example, "_____ takes the red tinge out of hair color while _____ removes green tones in blonding."

Headlines and Checklists

A headline is a short phrase or sentence that catches the reader's attention. Newspapers and magazines use catchy headlines to attract readers to their articles. Headlines can also guide note taking and serve as checklists for observation in field trips, role plays, and hands-on activities.

Choose words that communicate the most information with the most "punch" in the least amount of space. The participants should understand the words used. Headlines may start with an imperative or an action verb; or they may list the parts of an apparatus requiring a simple action, such as "Press Button A." Avoid qualifiers, pronouns, and articles unless they are crucial to identifying a specific part of a product. Use strong verbs. If the verb is "be" or "does," leave it out. Short phrases are easier to read because the information they contain is not buried among elaborate descriptions or extraneous adjectives. Participants may be distracted from the training session or discussion if they are trying to figure out a handout. Setting down information in one's own words facilitates the translation of ideas from trainer to learner.

Prepared guides to note taking can range from blank sheets of paper to transcriptions of presentations. Of course, blank sheets do not encourage or guide note taking. Only the disciplined person may jot down some of the information. At minimum, a note-taking guide should be one word: the skill, concept, or task.

While a transcription of a presentation may be a handy reference, it is of little use during the presentation. It is difficult to look up definitions or how-tos from a transcript. At worst, it can eliminate the need for the presentation altogether. If all of the information can be learned through reading, an alternative to a training session probably would be a better way of dispensing the information. Transcriptions could follow a speech or lecture but not a participative seminar.

A better way of writing note-taking guides is to use phrases, questions, or fill-in-the-blank statements. Use one or more pages for each main point. The title should summarize the main point, and the words or phrases on the page should summarize the subcategories that relate to the main point. Leave ample writing space after each word or phrase. A series of headlines can serve as observer checklists for role plays or hands-on applications. The addition of a grid often enhances checklists. For example, a grid may list particular behaviors to look for on the horizontal axis and locations that the behaviors occur on the vertical axis. A role-play checklist could list important skills that a coach should notice on the horizontal axis and the names or rounds of the role plays on the vertical axis. See the sample checklist in Figure 6-2.

	Round 1	Round 2	Round 3
Calls Out Prices			
Example:			
Gives customer choice of bags			
Example:			
Offer special services			
Example:			
Thanks the customer			
Example:			

Figure 6-2. Sample Role-Play Checklist: Supermarket Customer-Service Observer Sheet

Job Aids

Job aids are resources that people can use to help them do their jobs more quickly, accurately, and efficiently. Training designers can supply participants with job aids that they can take with them to help them remember what they have learned back on the job. The designer could write the steps of a procedure on small cards that participants can carry with them or post on their equipment, tools, or computers.

Laminated charts or lists can be attached to desks or counters. See Figure 6-3 for a sample job aid. Similarly, a job aid can serve as a troubleshooting device. Write the troubleshooting aids in a series of if/then statements. Below is an example of a troubleshooting job aid.

If *no video picture:*   Turn to channel 3;
                         Check cable connection; and
                         Turn master switch off and on.

Cash Register Turn-On Procedure

1. Turn on switch for bank of cash registers at #2.

2. Turn on switch for individual register (bottom left).

3. Unlock register drawer.

4. Initial register tape.

5. Count and verify opening dollar amounts and record on log.

Figure 6-3. Sample Job Aid

Scenarios

Scenarios are longer handouts with several paragraphs— sometimes several pages—describing situations that are used for case studies or role plays. As with all handouts, scenarios should not be too wordy; however, the descriptions and background information in a scenario are more detailed. Occasionally, the training designer will include instructions for participants to read an article, book chapter, or reference in a workshop. This is especially helpful if the participants have been too busy on the job to take the time to read. Make this reading an interactive activity. Case studies work best in training sessions if they are approximately one page in length. Case studies should be no longer than five pages unless the intent is to have the participants spend several hours on that case. Write direct, clear sentences that use action verbs. Avoid the passive voice. Separate the sentences into paragraphs of about three sentences each, based on the topic. Include dialog if desired, and be sure that readers will be able to tell who is speaking.

How to Find Material for Scenarios

Material for case-study or role-play scenarios can be gleaned from needs assessments—particularly if the needs assessment included observations or interviews. The designer can combine several incidents into one fictionalized one. Be sure that, if a real-life observation or incident is chosen, the names and any identifying details are changed to protect the parties involved.

How to Write a Scenario

Think of an incident that has either a finite beginning and end or that can be written that way. Take, for example, a conflict between employees. Start out with a sentence or two describing the employees—their ages, length of employment, attitudes toward their jobs, and their likes and dislikes. How did the conflict start? Without going into too much detail about the conflicting employees' relationship, what led up to the conflict? Describe the actual conflict. Where was it? What did the employees say and do? Create actual or made-up dialog. Finally, choose whether to reveal the outcome of the conflict or whether to ask the participants to guess at the outcome.

The possibilities for a scenario are almost endless, limited only by the requirements of the learning activity. Participants can create a simulation of a financial or organizational system. Fictionalized competitors' statistics can be created to give the participants experience in developing strategies. The designer can create profit-and-loss statements for a time period, then the trainer can ask the participants to plan a budget.

The directions and questions that accompany case studies follow the same format as the directions and questions for other learning activities. The following section presents a sample case study.

Sample Case Study

Instructions: The purpose of the following case study is to give you the opportunity to practice negotiating. Read this case and decide how you would handle the employees involved.

You are an area manager who oversees several branches of a temporary-employment organization. The following incident took place at one of your branches.

Barbara Metzger, a newly promoted branch manager, is a hard worker and has implemented several ideas for bringing in new accounts. Recently, you have advised Barbara to delegate more of her work. You also have been working with her to help her to be more sensitive toward her employees. Barbara has called you because she wants your support in giving a written warning to a new employee. She says:

> "Last night I was busy writing reports and trying to close the office, and I had a client on the phone. Terry interrupted me, saying something about a car out front. I suggested that Terry add up some accounts for me until I could talk with him. Terry started yelling and acted very rude. If it were up to me, I would fire him. However, I'm willing to settle for giving Terry a written warning about insubordination."

You have told Barbara that you want to talk to Terry before you make up your mind. Terry Newhouse is a new clerk who has been with the branch for six months. He is very intelligent and you believe that he has quite a bit of potential. You would like to make him a management trainee, but he has appeared a bit timid. Therefore, you have advised him to speak up more as a way of demonstrating leadership potential. When questioned about the incident, Terry says:

> "Last night when I left, I was driving down the street right in front of the branch when a car pulled out in front of me and hit me. I wasn't hurt, but my car was no longer drivable. I walked back to the branch to ask Barbara for help, but she wouldn't even talk to me and gave me more work to do. I was upset and spoke up to her, just as you suggested. Then I left to find someone who would help me with my car."

A written activity, a discussion, or a role play could be designed to accompany the preceding case study.

In another type of role play, participants are asked to think of their own scenarios. For example: "Think of a conflict between two employees that you have handled recently or that you will be asked to handle. First, tell your group about the details of the incident; then, two people in the group will role play the conflicting employees. Using the negotiation skills that you've just learned, try to resolve the conflict."

The designer can combine a scenario with directions and checklists to create a complete handout packet with case studies and role plays. Remember to include enough information with each scenario so that the players know something about each role and where and when the action occurs.

CHAPTER SUMMARY

Written materials that learners read during seminars, peruse on their own, or carry away to use as references, are basic elements of most types of training. Participant handouts should be concise and written in a style that the participants will understand in order to be most effective and useful. Five elements are basic to most participant handouts, overheads, and work sheets:

- Directions;
- Questions;
- Fill-in-the-blank statements;
- Headlines; and
- Scenarios.

7

WRITING VIDEOSCRIPTS

Loren received the difficult assignment of developing a literacy-training program for entry-level workers in a public-utilities organization. He chose to use videos for the training, because it would be difficult to find and train trainers to be literacy tutors. Loren thought that video would enable him to reach more people in a wider range of locations without the expense of bringing them to a training center or sending trainers to various work sites. And, of course, because the employees being trained could not read, written material was useless. Video seemed the best medium.

Loren interviewed the employees who could not read or write well enough to fill out applications. Through his prework, he found that most of the employees who needed literacy training had a second-grade reading level. They could recognize a few simple words, knew numbers, and could write their names.

Loren previously had taught remedial reading to high school students, so he felt he was qualified to do literacy training. He did research and obtained more information from the *Laubach Way to Reading* series (1983). Loren planned to host and narrate his videos, in which he would explain how to sound out words the way he had done in the classroom.

Loren's supervisor, who had attended several video-lecture courses in college, approved the project. He agreed with

Loren's theory that people who are unable to read could benefit the most from videotaped training. Loren's major objective was to bring the participants to at least a sixth-grade reading level. He proposed several modules that focused on phonics—especially on recognizing vowel sounds. Loren decided to pilot one module first to test his video concept. Figure 7-1 is an except from Loren's script.

Narrator: Hello. Today we will review the long "a" sound. It is spelled in four main ways. One way sounds just like the letter "a," as in "paper."

(*Show the letter "A," the word "paper," and a newspaper.*)

Narrator: This word is *paper*. The first vowel sound is a long "a." It is written "a." Read these words.

(*Pause as the following words are shown separately:* David, April, baby, lady, table, radio. *Then show each word again.*)

Figure 7-1. Excerpt from Loren's Videoscript

If we continued with Loren's script, we would see that the narrator read to the audience several words (David, April, baby, table) that used "a" to indicate the long "a" sound. Then the narrator read a short story using the words while the page from the story was visible on the screen— with the key words highlighted. The narrator also asked questions and suggested that the viewers write down some of the words.

The technical crew videotaped and edited Loren's presentation for the pilot module. Five employees, who had been tested and found to need reading improvement, watched the hour-long video. One of them fell asleep; the others yawned and appeared to doze. The employees did not answer the questions that the video asked them; they simply kept the videotape running. The video did not appear to help them learn to write and read. Determined, Loren continued the tests with other groups.

Managers liked the video format because it did not involve them. They could leave their employees in front of the monitor. But after a few showings of the video, many managers saw no results and stopped showing it. The employees who watched it complained about how boring it was, which made the other employees dread the literacy training.

Obviously, something went wrong with Loren's training—something that was difficult to pinpoint. Loren's reasoning for choosing video was sound, and he was experienced with the subject matter. What Loren needed was a *more interesting* video—something containing more than himself speaking a script. He needed something to catch the viewers' attention and to keep them interested—enticing them to learn. The employees needed to learn skills that they could immediately use on the job. Handouts could and should have accompanied the video, because the trainees needed to learn to read writing on paper as well as on a screen.

The video medium, to be effective, must diverge in many ways from classroom-style training. One of the main differences between classroom learning and video learning is that a class can be lengthy, while a video must be short. One hour of nonstop video is far too long. Ten-minute video segments are most effective. Rather than using a classroom-teacher model, pattern educational videos after television commercials.

Within the ten or so minutes of the video segment, the pace should be fast. The audience should see a great variety of images that change every few seconds. Watching a person talking or lecturing on video is draining and requires more concentration than even an in-person lecture. Many people who have grown up with television have not mastered prolonged concentration; on television, commercial breaks take place every ten to fifteen minutes.

Training videos should be a *Sesame Street* for adults. They should contain a great deal of repetition, which should be enacted in different ways and should be connected with mnemonic devices such as pictures, characters, jingles, and music.

Keep in mind, also, that video is a passive media. Loren made the mistake of attempting some interaction with viewers through his videotaped questions and through his directions to the viewers to read and write. Actually, basic-skills training requires that the learners receive a great deal of personal attention and encouragement, because a person's lack of skill in such a basic area is often accompanied by a low self-image. And one thing that a video does not offer is personal attention.

Loren also tried to use the video in ineffective and awkward ways. When he had participants try to read many words from the screen, for example, he not only strained the viewers' eyesight but he made them *not* want to complete the task.

Most training designers are not required to be expert technicians as well. Instead, they would usually work closely with people who possess expertise about camera angles, editing, special effects, sound, and lighting. The job of the designer is to ensure that the video meets the training objectives and that the writing and/or script is clear and well written. Corporate videoscript writers may also write scripts to sell products, to publicize, or to entertain. This book will be less concerned with these three objectives. A music video or an eye opener may be used to start a training session, but it alone does not constitute a training video.

HOW TO WRITE THE TRAINING VIDEO

Many of the methods for designing audiovisual aids can be applied to the writing of the videoscript. Some training videos can stand alone, but most will be more effective if they can be combined with viewer-trainer interaction. Marked turn-off points in the videotape, at which time the viewers are asked to respond, can be very strong training, but most people tend not to do this without a facilitator. Use video to show and explain something that cannot be brought into the classroom—to listen to an expert discussing a topic or to view something located halfway around the world, for example. Similarly, video training can ask questions to be used with viewer handouts or with discussions. The video can interact or role play with the viewers and can form the basis for a learning activity.

Videoscripts employ four basic types of writing: *visuals, narration, dialog,* and *screen words* (also known as *burn-ins*). These are built around various frameworks, often modeled after those used in television programing and helpful in preparing the script.

Framework

Before the script writing can begin, the writer needs to select a framework (the theme that holds the variety together). On the one hand, the video will need a great deal of variety with changes every few seconds to grab and hold the viewers' attention. On the other hand, a video needs a continuing theme that holds the pieces together. Television, particularly the commercials, can inspire ideas for training videos. A training video can present concepts and skills through the following types of formats:

- *Documentaries,* such as tours or "History of..." programs;
- *Testimonials* (interviews, possibly based on a talk-show or newscast format);
- *Dramas* (serious or funny); and
- Other entertainment formats.

The format should not detract from the learning. If viewers pay more attention to a clown than to what the clown is doing with the spreadsheet, the video is not serving its purpose.

Writing a framework helps in planning and communicates the purpose of the video to others. In the training map or proposal, write a simple statement about the content of the video, relating objective concepts and facts to the video framework. For example: This drama shows a person using all the steps of CPR (cardio-pulmonary resuscitation) to save a person's life. The training concepts are the CPR steps. The framework is the documentary.

If the training video has a story line, such as in a drama or documentary, Syd Field (1984) recommends that the video begin by stating the story line in terms of a character and an action. For example: "A nurse reorganizes the routine of her division to be more patient oriented." This will help to focus and guide the writing.

Next, the designer should create an outline or an expanded version of an outline called a *treatment*. The treatment describes what happens in each scene, what the viewers will see, and how the scenes should affect the viewers. A treatment can be presented in narrative form, or it could be outlined as the sample in Figure 7-2. It should answer questions such as, "Will they be puzzled, surprised, curious, or informed? Will they be intrigued and want to know more? Will they understand the importance and the mechanics of certain jobs? Will they feel good about wanting to improve?"

Visuals	Information	Audience
1. Boy riding bicycle in a neighborhood, having fun	Title and Intro	Joy of riding a bike
2. On-camera narrator as boy straddles and pushes off	How to get started	Knowledge of starting bicycle
3. Diagrams of balancing; boy leaning	Explanation of balancing	Feeling confident about not falling
4. Boy stops bike; brake shown	How to stop, how brakes work	Understanding how to control and get off bike

Figure 7-2.   Excerpt from treatment on "How to Ride a Bicycle"

Instead of his dull, one-man video presentation, Loren could have developed a story about a person learning to read, a documentary about several new readers, or an entertaining television-commercial-type show of dancing letters, words, and sentences. Choosing a framework is the first step in writing a script. Next, write a treatment or outline to present to management, clients, etc., for approval, which will guide the writing. The script can then be written from the outline, starting with the visuals that have been sketched out in the treatment.

Visuals

Visuals are what the camera and the viewers see on the screen. They should be the start of the script in terms of how the video designer should think. Think in sights and sounds rather than in words. Then, write descriptions of the scenes, views, and images in your mind. Visuals comprise the main portion of the message in a video. Visuals are more than just pictures—they are moving pictures. Cameras angle, scenes change, characters or narrators move about, or all three. Designers need to consider what would be going on if the characters were not talking.

Of course, writers should first put visuals into words because of the nature of video—if the program were all talk, an audiotape or a live speaker could accomplish its goals just as well. Video should be chosen as the medium for a training program because the training requires that the participants see something that cannot physically be brought into the training site.

As a designer writes a videoscript, he or she should continually strive to answer the following question: "What do we see?" The designer can leave camera angles, lighting, and special effects to the production crew, or he or she can include them. However, a designer should not leave all of the visual effects up to the producers; this is a sign that the designer is not visualizing what is happening thoroughly enough. Designers should describe what they see, but not in so much detail that it locks the production crew into an inflexible schedule. Describe enough of the action, the scene, and the mood for crew and audience to know what is going on. Too much detail will make the script too long and too difficult to read. The average visual is a paragraph long. It sometimes is written in full sentences, but more often consists of fragments. These phrases become more vivid when the writer uses comparisons and states what feeling should be conveyed. Fragments are comprised mainly of adjectives and action verbs.

Settings

Every video must have a *setting*, which orients the viewers to the video's time, place, and circumstance in history. The setting can establish what is going on or when the process does not involve people. The shots that establish the setting usually occur at the beginning of scenes. When creating a setting, the designer should bear in mind which details are most crucial to the development of the training. Does the action take place inside or outside? What time of day is it? What is happening?

Describe the building or locale. How close or far away are the viewers? Should any things be in plain sight, such as a sign, a label, a title, or a newspaper headline? Instead of writing, "The scene takes place outside an office building," think in more detail. Without describing the bricks and doors, indicate whether the building is ornate, rundown, or a high-rise. The setting can be very clear with only a few seconds of visuals. Similarly, interiors can be clear in a short time. Make sure that viewers will be able to tell what room they are looking at and what part of the room the characters are in. Writers often find it helpful to write at the scene. Visual aids can be used in the video itself. For example, maps or diagrams can help viewers visualize a travel route. The narrator can point to places on a map; a more sophisticated map could light up in different locations as the narrator talks about each one. Be creative in inventing unusual visuals to hold the viewers' attention. Animation, costumes, unusual juxtaposition of objects in a scene—all can convey messages. Use simple details that communicate without words; a close-up of hands pouring aspirin from a bottle, for example, can be very revealing of character.

Designers should spell out any sort of explanation of a process in the clearest terms possible. Some videos, of course, show views or processes that are not usually visible (e.g., a magnified view of blood cells or a cutaway view of a machine in operation). These must either be described thoroughly or, even better, illustrated with diagrams and drawings known as *story boards*.

Montages

Montages are rapid sequences of short scenes that often are compiled from stock footage of previously completed videotape. Often, videoscript writers simply indicate where montages should be inserted, even referring to each montage by number. If new footage is needed, the writer should prepare a general description of the desired shot and effect. An example of a montage is several different shots of people at a counter helping customers and answering phones. The effect could be a feeling that we are seeing a busy, productive office. Another type of montage could be various shots of a machine's moving parts. Montages can also show histories, with several people, places, and symbols linked in creative ways. Montages often introduce a training video or summarize all of the parts of a training session.

Characters

The videoscript writer must also describe the people who appear in the video and their roles. When characters first appear on the screen, give a brief description of each one. Describe only the characteristics necessary for the video production. Sometimes a character must wear a certain type of clothes (e.g., an army uniform), must have a certain hairstyle, or must be seen with certain props. For example, a video whose purpose is to teach people who sell liquor may specify the following type of character: *Young male of uncertain age—it is difficult to tell whether or not he is twenty-one.*

More important than the characters' appearance are their actions. Use their actions and the way they talk to characterize them rather than have the actors or a narrator describe them. Sometimes the body language is important, particularly in videos that train for better communication or if a story line is the training vehicle. A typical action line may be, "Eyebrows raised, he looks over his left shoulder."

Sometimes the videoscript writer intersperses scenes and people by using the character's point of view. For example, we see Jay as he moves his chair back, stands up, and then looks out the window. Then we switch to the scene that Jay is watching—his point of view (indicated in Hollywood scripts as "Jay's POV"). We see smoke rising from one of the cars in a big parking garage. Then we go back to Jay as he quickly sits down. The next scene is only Jay's hand as it reaches for the telephone.

Details can tell the audience many things about the character. We should see the character from several viewpoints: head, whole body, and details that reveal or symbolize something, such as the drops of sweat on a forehead.

Loren needed more than the narrator's head and the words on the screen. He could have scripted visuals in a variety of settings and described different people. Perhaps even montages could have helped. After you write visuals, then write the narration or dialog.

Narration

A narrator verbally explains concepts and training points in connection with what the video shows. Avoid overwriting this part. If the visuals obviously show something, there is often no need to have the narrator say it. Nevertheless, it may be important for the narrator to repeat the visuals with training concepts and skills, because the repetition doubles the chance of getting them across. Let the moving picture speak for itself while the narrator enhances or complements what cannot be shown.

Narration is one of the most common training video techniques. With narration, you not only can explain a process, but you can connect a series of interviews or montages. The narrator transitions among these.

The narrator can be on camera or off or a combination. With a story line, the off-camera narrator is the main character who tells about himself or herself in a flashback or another setting. In other frameworks, the off-camera narrator assumes a godlike position, but you can write the words to describe impartially in the third person. The third person usually informs viewers in a documentary style. Or the narrator can be an enthusiastic insider who says "we."

Write the off-camera narration after the footage has been shot. This is particularly true if the footage consists of live interviews in which there are specific topics, but you do not know ahead of time what the people being interviewed will say. Write the narration that glues these interviews into a continuous flow. Choose important segments of the interviews. The script will then be a transcription of the interview segments and the narrative connection.

Narrators who represent someone in the workplace are usually on camera. Sometimes they have definite roles, such as the employee who describes what he or she does, or an expert, like a doctor or a manager, who points out the skills of several employees. The on-camera narrator speaks to the camera.

The on-camera narrator can also be a stand-up comedian who bumbles or jokes to explain the points. The audience needs to be very clear about when the joker is serious and when the lines are only a joke. The outsider on-camera narrator can also be like a newscaster or sportscaster who reports play by play.

When you write narration, you do not have to write complete sentences. A narrator sometimes may label parts, no need to write, "This is..." Short, simple headlines work best. Use active verbs and remove all unnecessary words. Use words that are easy to pronounce, so the narrator will not become entangled in a tongue twister. Write for out-loud readability. Intricate sentences will not work.

Loren's narrator was on camera when explaining sounds and off camera when reading words. Dialog could vary his two dry choices.

Dialog with Two Narrators

Dialog has many uses in training videos, in an explanation of a concept or task. Two-person narration, videos demonstrating communication skills, and dramas all require dialog. To write dialog, write the way people talk, but more succinctly and toward training points.

Just having two people and two voices instead of one adds greater variety and keeps viewers' attention longer. Adding another voice and person in Loren's script would be an easy addition to make. The two narrators can be on camera in the work place, or we can just hear their voices as the task is shown in action; or we could have a combination of these.

In Figure 7-3, the first narrator makes a statement about a skill. Then the other responds to elaborate, give an example, or disagree with an alternative.

When the two narrators have different points of view and disagree or debate an issue, the argument can convince

---

Narrator 1: Word processing is easy to learn.

Narrator 2: That is, *some* word-processing programs are. We are going to demonstrate several.

Narrator 1: I presume you will include *WORD*.

Figure 7-3. Sample Script with Two Narrators

audiences of a certain procedure or can inform them that they can use several different procedures and under what circumstances one works better than another. Fewer questions occur in this format; more opinions and feelings. Script the characters to speak from the "I": "I feel," and "I believe." They might even say, "You should." See Figure 7-4 for an example.

Interviews

Interviews give another alternative to a narrative explanation. The interview is between an outsider or naive character and an expert. The expert can be real or an actor. Similarly, the questioning character could be a professional interviewer, a new employee, or even a supervisor who asks how the employee does the work. Sometimes the expert is just in a studio, but you will add greater interest if the expert is on the job or actually using the products. A news format or a talk show add yet another variation of the interview.

Write questions that the interviewer asks. These questions resemble the questions that you wrote for needs assessments, particularly those for information-gathering interviews, the "W's." The difference is that now you know the answers, so you want to write questions that target the main learning points so the training video interviews lead the expert to explain the main points.

Notice the questions used on news interviews and talk shows. Video-interview questions also differ from needs-assessment interview questions in that you will not always write a whole-sentence question. The interviewer will say phrases to prompt the expert.

Doctor 1: In my clinic, each clerk specializes: in scheduling patients or in billing or in assisting my nurse. I find this more efficient.

Doctor 2: I don't think that's a good idea, because it keeps patients waiting. In my clinic, I make sure everyone knows how to do every job.

Doctor 1: You should try it my way. You'll be surprised how smoothly things run.

Figure 7-4. Sample Script Using "I" and "You Should"

A video can model job interviews or employer-employee patterns, such as motivation, instruction-giving, listening, and suggesting ideas. It can also show how to and how not to relate to customers and clients, to community leaders, and to other businesses. How to lead a meeting or make a training presentation can also be shown with video.

Conversational Dialog

Compose conversations that showcase use or misuse of the skills to be trained. Write a focused back-and-forth discussion in which characters use the skills, such as confronting a late employee.

Training that uses a story usually includes dialog among several people. The dialog contributes to the development of the story and will often include individual expression.

Write a variety of sentences, not only questions and statements, but also exclamations, as in Figure 7-5.

John walks into office, mumbling.

John: How I hate this job! Another day of nothing but problems.

John sits at the desk and just stares. Co-worker, Jerry, sticks his head in the door.

Jerry: John?

John: (angrily) What do you want?

Jerry: Sorrryyyy!

Figure 7-5. Sample Dialog with Expression

One way that dialog writing differs from formal writing is that often the sentences are incomplete. They will be phrases, even sounds: "What customers?" "Ugh, bad news."

If you want characters to have a unique personality, give them phrases that they repeat, such as "Oh, you guys!" Be careful, however, not to allow personalities to detract from the learning.

In writing dialog, use the words that people in the work place use. Use short blocks of dialog for each character. Do not write in dialect, such as a southern drawl, because it is too difficult to read. If dialect is necessary, like a down-home style, include instructions and leave it up to the actors.

A good practice for writing dialog is to record in writing actual dialog as it's happening. As you overhear a conversation, document it word for word. Try this two or three times with different conversations. You might even want to do this in the work place. Then analyze what you recorded. Cut out the unnecessary words and boring trivia; make your dialog sound like conversation, but make it more interesting and informative.

WRITING CAPTIONS

In addition to writing visuals, narration, and dialog, you may write words, sentences, or questions that appear on the screen for viewers to read. Sometimes these words reinforce training points, and sometimes words on the screen help make the video interactive. Loren went too far when he put the pages of an entire story on the screen.

Words on the screen can label the concept or procedure that you want to teach. You can write a title to the whole program and titles to the parts that appear on special screens with colored backgrounds, or you can superimpose the words over the action. Technicians refer to this latter process as "burn-in." In the script on a separate line, write "burn-in" and the words. Burn-ins with arrows can point to parts of a machine or process. For example, if you are scripting a video that shows how to negotiate a fee with a consultant, as we see a manager and consultant interact, label each part of the negotiation process.

You can make the video more interactive by asking the audience questions. At the beginning, you could have the actor or narrator say that the audience should look for something. It could be similar to "what's wrong with this picture?" Reinforce the search with words on the screen, such as "LOOK FOR MISTAKES" or "STOP. TURN OFF THE VIDEO UNTIL YOU HAVE ANSWERED THE TRAINER'S QUESTIONS."

You can have the audience answer in seminar discussions or record their answers on handouts. Then the video can show the answer. With interactive video, viewers can answer the video via a computer, whether by keyboard, touch screen, or mouse. In that case, you will not only write questions, but you may post choices of answers on the screen. You will also need to script responses to right or wrong answers.

If you are required to author CAI (Computer Assisted Instruction) or CBT (Computer Based Training), which also requires mastering authoring commands, you will need to write text, questions, answers, and responses to answers. In using CAI for learning computer applications, you can direct learners from a box on the screen.

In a box on the screen or at the top or bottom of the screen, direct learners on what to do. If instructions are longer than three or four sentences, books or handouts should accompany the program instead of so much written material on the screen. This reduces eye strain and gives students easy access to reference material.

You will need to write responses, so students will know how they did. For every answer, avoid being too negative. Indicate what part was inaccurate and advise them to try again.

Right answers have several possibilities, and it is best to vary the response. Sometimes it is feasible to tell students what they did right, such as "Good answer. The patient screen is complete and accurate." Look for several ways to write that the answer is correct. For example, "Great job!" "Perfect answer!" "You got it right!"

Words on the screen can range from titles and burn-ins to questions to a whole series of nothing but words. Write these briefly, but in a way that promotes maximum learning.

CHAPTER SUMMARY

You will improve the quality of training ideas with a written script instead of just videotaping training or a job in action. Write what the viewers should see. Also script what actors and narrators say with to-the-point dialog that sounds the way people talk. You will also need to write words that appear on the screen to emphasize the training points. With CAI or interactive video, you will need to write text, questions, and responses that appear on the screen. A training video will have the following parts:

- Visuals
- Narration
- Dialog
- Words on the screen

Evaluations and measurements will let you know the results of your written materials.

REFERENCES

Field, S. (1984). *Screen writers' workbook*. New York: Dell.

Laubach, F.C., Kirk, E.M., & Laubach, R.S. (1983). *The Laubach way to reading (Skill Book 3)*. Syracuse, NY: New Readers Press.

8

WRITING EVALUATIONS AND MEASUREMENTS

Shawn, a trainer at Waring Distributors, also designed training programs. Waring sold clothing and housewares, primarily through catalogs and mail orders, but also through several wholesale and retail outlets throughout the United States. The original purpose of Shawn's position was to improve customer service.

Shawn had worked with other retailers and corporations on customer service before, so she customized several kinds of programs. Her research showed that customers wanted speed and knowledgeable employees. The employees wanted to know what they were expected to do and to get feedback and pats on the back for doing it. Managers needed help in developing systems that supported the service and in carrying out the systems.

Shawn outlined training for managers that included problem solving, empowerment, and solving employee problems. She also outlined a basic customer-service training for everyone. She brought in an expert in time-motion studies who taught them how to be more efficient. Waring executives approved her map.

Shawn started with managers and helped them to develop systems for improving customer service, helpfulness, and friendliness, that would include rewards and accountability. She trained them to observe, evaluate, and follow up on customer service as employees served. The training for all employees taught them how to speak with better telephone voices and how to smile and greet customers, using their names. She made sure each employee understood the entire operation, the location of products, and how helping customers fit in with the bigger picture.

Shawn designed discussions so all employees had a chance to discuss and contribute their ideas at the training meetings. She also created several activities in which all employees tried responding to telephone calls that Shawn made through audiotapes. They role played handling several kinds of customers, and they brainstormed how they could help one another.

The managers used several case studies for practicing motivating and making employees accountable. They also role played complimenting, encouraging, and giving negative feedback to employees.

Wonderful workbooks that looked like magazines, with color photos, guided all Waring employees through training. Many overhead slides and flip charts matched. The workbook looked so nice, that it enticed Waring employees to look at it again on their own time and even to show it to their families.

Waring employees came away with a new understanding of the company, their jobs, and what they should do to get better. Job aids that attached to telephones, cash registers, and the mail-order area reminded them of the three C's of service. And the Waring employees felt good about helping customers.

Similarly, managers carried cards in their pockets that reviewed the problem-solving and employee-relations skills that could help them carry out the new service systems. Everyone seemed pleased, so Shawn went to her superiors, eager to develop the training function and spread customer service. She asked, "How did I do?"

She was shocked when the Waring vice president replied, "You tell us." They wanted her to prove to them that the expenditure on training had made a difference. She was not sure how she could do this.

Training can be evaluated on four different levels. The most common asks participants how they liked the training sessions. Sometimes called smile sheets, participants fill these out at a seminar or shortly thereafter. More sophisticated measures include pretests and posttests, which assess participants' knowledge and skills as they change. Further measures delve into changes in job performances and impacts on the bottom line. The writing of these measures parallels many of the surveys you wrote for needs assessment. What you want to measure goes back to objectives. Evaluation asks, "Did I achieve the objectives?" See Dixon (1990) and Mager (1973) for more details. Evaluations also become needs assessments for subsequent training.

OPINION EVALUATIONS

One of the most common ways that training departments evaluate training is by asking for participants' opinions. Participants may fill out a form as the last part of training, or the trainers may send out the evaluation a few days after training and ask the participants to return it. The response rates tend to be very low.

The reason evaluations are sometimes referred to as "smile sheets" is that the most common type of question is whether the participants liked the training, and the answers tend to be positive. In addition to asking about their likes and dislikes, an evaluation may ask what they learned, what stimulated thinking, what they expect to use, how the presentation could be improved, and what future training programs they would like to have. The sheet may reference the training session as a whole or ask one or more questions about each training topic. Two pages should be the maximum so that participants are not taxed. In creating an evaluation form, first write some brief instructions. Then write open-ended questions about topics or provide sentences that need completing or statements that need rating.

Instructions

Use the imperative to guide participants to be honest and to tell them how much and why they should fill this out. An example would be, "Please help us improve our training sessions for you. Answer each question in an open, honest way with a few short sentences." Most evaluations are anonymous, to help solicit revealing answers. If you decide that you want respondents' names, perhaps because you want to follow up with them, you should indicate that in the instructions. Also include a line or space for names on the sheet.

Open-Ended Questions

The general instructions may ask a question, followed by a list of topics; for example, "Please tell us, in a few words: What did you like about the subjects?" Another question might be, "How could we improve them?" Alternatively, you could write a question in general and then questions about each topic. When you make the questions open-ended, you benefit from the participants' own words as answers. This technique is less likely to lead them to an answer and may give you some ideas that you did not expect. Use verbs such as "like, dislike, improve." Figure 8-1 provides some sample questions.

Sentence Completion

You can get similar information with sentence completion, which is another way to stimulate the participants' thinking about the training. Figure 8-2 provides examples of the sentence-completion type of evaluation.

What did you like best?

What was least useful to you?

How could we improve the program?

What topics would you like to see in the future?

Figure 8-1. Sample Questions from Typical Evaluation Form

Sentence completions and open-ended questions will generate a variety of responses. These can be coded and the frequencies counted.

I learned the most about...

When I'm back on the job, I'll...

The presenters were best at...

Because of this seminar, I'm going to change...

Figure 8-2. Sample To-Be-Completed Sentences.

Ratings

For more scientific feedback, ask participants to rate parts of training seminars according to what they learned or gained, what they liked, what they found useful, or other criteria that we discussed before. Do this when you want to compare evaluations, either among groups or among time spans. Clarify what they are rating. A scale often works better than the other methods, because ratings by different participants are easier to compare. Figure 8-3 illustrates the rating method.

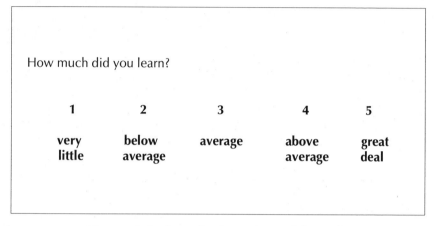

How much did you learn?

1	2	3	4	5
very little	below average	average	above average	great deal

Figure 8-3. Sample Question with Scale

An odd number (i.e., three, five, seven, or nine) of choices allows the respondents to choose a middle ground; sometimes you may prefer to force them to choose one side or the other. Because these evaluations are opinions, they do not tell you how much the participants really learned nor how they will use the information. They just tell you a subjective amount that the participants estimate. To get more information about what they really learned, you will need a test.

TESTS

Another way to evaluate a training program is to test the participants' knowledge. Tests get closer to telling whether the training met the learning objectives, at least in terms of knowledge. A pencil-and-paper test can reveal how much participants learned, but it does not tell you if they can or will use the skills on the job. The best way to discover if the employees learned from the training session is to give the same test at the start of the session and at the end. Pretests and posttests have the advantage of proving that your design made a difference.

Educational tests can be divided into two main categories: subjective and objective. Subjective tests may include essays and short answers. Skills such as writing, decision making, and other communication skills may be better tested by subjective tests. Essays can be based on case studies and some of the other activities discussed in Chapter 5. For example, if you provide data on demands, daily receipts, and costs over a month, then you may ask students, "Based on this information, write a proposal requesting additional help."

However, subjective tests are extremely difficult to grade, especially for those without a background in education, and it is almost impossible to be consistent in grading them. Some ways to help trainers grade essay tests include providing guides to evaluating written materials such as "Look for these points and count how many times each appear."

Objective tests have the advantage of being consistent and easy to grade. If you find that learners consistently miss the same question, either the designer needs to improve the question or the training did not effectively cover that topic. Objective tests include fill-in-the-blank, true-false, matching, and multiple-choice items.

Fill-in-the-blank items form a continuum between short answers and objective tests. For these, write sentences that have a word or phrase omitted. The way to write these directly parallels the way you wrote guides for note-taking fill-in-the-blank sentences (see Chapter 5). For the test grader, you will need to include a list of possible answers on a test key. Since fill-in-the-blank items have the disadvantage of having many possible answers, you may not be able to list them all. More objective tests require one right answer.

True-false tests consist of statements that students evaluate. You can take the true-false statements directly from the facilitator's dialog in the design. Leave the statement as is if you want it to be true, and change key points if the statement is to be false.

A major problem with true-false statements is that taken out of context, they can have multiple interpretations. True-false items work better with very precise, unquestionable statements. Avoid using definitive words such as "always, never, only," because they rarely can be true.

A multiple-choice test overcomes the difficulties of subjective and true-false tests. Because of multiple choice advantages, educators use this form of test more than any other. Multiple-choice items avoid the absolutes of true-false by giving several options.

For multiple-choice items, write a question or a statement to be completed. Fill-in-the-blank items can also work as multiple-choice items. Use the part of the statement that gets repeated as the main stem rather than repeating it with each choice. If you are asking about a definition, put the definition in the stem. Make the question or statement straightforward and simple, not compound or complex. Include conditions necessary about the question; but otherwise, leave out unnecessary words, particularly adjectives, adverbs, and phrases.

It is more difficult to create wrong choices, because you want possible answers without giving away the correct answers. An excellent way to acquire the various answers is first to ask open-ended questions or fill-in statements and see what learners typically answer. The choices should be common misconceptions or errors that you know from the needs assessment.

Choices should be distinct from one another and not overlap. Also, write parallel choices; that is, if the correct choice is a noun, the other choices should be nouns; or if the correct choice begins with a verb, the other choices should begin with a verb. Be sure to mix the location of the right answer—not always B, for example. Figure 8-4 provides a sample multiple-choice question. In that sample, the card would display all the numbers in the choices.

Write from three to seven choices for each item. The more choices you write, the more difficult it will be to write good alternatives. Often all the questions in a single test have the same number of choices, but this consistency is not essential. The number of questions that you write depends on the complexity of the training topic and the amount of time that you want to give to a test. Your objectives should guide the number of test questions.

On the card you were given, which number is the directional code?

    a. 007
    b. 828-09-1112
    c. 5.9
    d. 1622

Figure 8-4. Sample Multiple-Choice Question

Avoid the negative multiple choice because it confuses test-takers. Negatives sometimes seem easier to write, but they lead you away from looking for good possible, but not accurate, choices. An example of a negative question is, "Which of these is <u>not</u> a filter?"

Unless you are thoroughly experienced in writing multiple-choice items, refrain from using combined answers, such as "c and d," "none of the above," and "all of the above." They are tricky to write well and usually turn out either more confusing than necessary, or they may give away the answer.

Matching tests are like extended multiple-choice items, except that the items are usually phrases or words rather than statements or questions. For example, states could be listed in one column; state capitals, in the other. You can use matching items for many tests, including dates, definitions, causes and effects, and labels on a diagram. It is better to have more responses in the matching column than the original, so that people taking the test cannot guess by elimination.

Subjective and objective tests measure the extent of knowledge gained in a training session. Most educators use multiple-choice tests because of their benefits over other types. Care needs to be taken in writing clearly understood stems and choices that attract possible, yet distinguishable answers. People sometimes do well on tests, but not on the job, or vice versa.

JOB EVALUATION

Tests tell whether people know the skills, but not whether they use them, particularly on the job. More practical tests work like driving tests; that is, the people actually perform the task. You can evaluate some skills with a practical, driving-like test; but with other skills, employees must be on the actual job to demonstrate their abilities. A more realistic evaluation occurs on the job—with all its other demands and interruptions—and yet another level of evaluation is to determine where the skills impact the profits and losses in an operation.

Practical Tests

Many of the activities suggested in Chapter 5 can also be tests to determine whether or not people can use skills. Use of skills with equipment can be tested in a classroom if the equipment is present. You can use the checklist again or you can go by the typing-test model—the number of words in a minute minus the number of errors. Another alternative is to look at the results. You can determine, for example, if the cake making or pipe fitting created a usable product. In any of these cases, you would need only to write directions for how to give the tests and include a checklist or score sheet to report on those who succeeded.

Just like they performed in a driving test, people can try out communication skills in role plays. In addition to writing the role play as you did for an activity, the checklist is essential for the person giving the test. The test checklist matches the activity checklist. It should list the skills, so the observers can check off each time the employee uses the skill.

The major problem with these kinds of tests in a classroom is that there is no way of knowing whether the employees use the skills on the job—where the environment differs. Just as you can give practical tests in a workshop, you can evaluate the employees even better by testing them later in the workplace. Evaluating on-the-job performance shows how employees both retain the skills and use them.

Job Performance

Many evaluation models boil down to two: (1) a comparison of two groups—one with and one without the training and (2) a comparison of the same group before and after training. The reason on-the-job performance less often gets tested is the expense and time needed for the testing. An outsider could observe, or you could ask managers, peers, or employees of a manager to fill out checklists or questionnaires. Or you could ask the learners themselves, but they are likely to be the most biased.

Construct observation checklists exactly the same way you did in Chapter 5 for seminar activities. Use objectives to guide you on the topics and number of items to check off. Frequency counts are easier and more reliable than measuring how well employees carried out each objective. Figure 8-5 provides a sample observation checklist.

The longer the list, the harder it could be to use. The impartial observer checklist works best in places that have public access. If a checklist is used in a closed area, such as a factory or the kitchen of a bakery, the observing itself can influence workers to be at their best.

A survey of managers, peers, or employees who work for the group targeted for training can also indicate changes as

Check each time a sales rep does each of the following
SALES REPS

	1	2	3
Demonstrates product			
Performs trial close			
Suggests related sales			

Figure 8-5. Sample Observation Checklist

a result of training. See Chapter 2 for a discussion of ways to write surveys. Figure 8-6 provides a sample evaluation of a supervisor's behavior. A change in the secretaries' responses before and after training would show that the supervisors' training made a difference and would also indicate where the training needed improving.

For assessing on-the-job performance, either write checklists, surveys, or tests that have already been discussed. For the impact of training on the bottom line, simply collect and report the data.

BOTTOM-LINE IMPACT

The ultimate test of a training program that owners and executives would like to see is an increase in profits and/or sales and a decrease in costs and losses. The trouble is that businesses do not operate in an experimental void where a researcher can control all the variables and say for sure that training caused the changes. What you can do is find out if a change occurred and suggest that training contributed to the change. Look at sales or other rates before training and then after.

You have little to write in this case because you are mostly looking at data that the organization normally tracks anyway. Measures more indirect than profit and loss include rates such as performance issues. It does not do any good to look at bottom-line results in connection with training if you do not also examine performance. If losses decreased but employees still were making errors that the training was designed to correct, the decrease would not be due to the training. Other measures might include defects or mistakes, complaints, special orders, absenteeism, tardiness, turnover, and sales or production per employee.

To Secretaries: Please circle a number that evaluates how often your supervisor does the following:

My supervisor:

Gives thorough direction for each new task

always	usually	sometimes	occasionally	never
1	2	3	4	5

Encourages me to ask questions

always	usually	sometimes	occasionally	never
1	2	3	4	5

Sends me to training when I need it

always	usually	sometimes	occasionally	never
1	2	3	4	5

Coaches me on how to improve

always	usually	sometimes	occasionally	never
1	2	3	4	5

**Figure 8-6. Sample Survey for Evaluating a
Supervisor's Behavior**

The report on these data could consist of a simple table that communicates to your client the success of the training program, such as the one illustrated in Table 8-1.

Table 8-1. Sample Table Showing Success of Training

Sales Per Employee		
	First Quarter TRAINING Second Quarter	
District A	7,500	10,000
District B	5,000	8,000
District C	6,000	7,500

As Robinson and Robinson (1989) well argue, for training to have an impact, the environment must support what employees learned in training.

CHAPTER SUMMARY

You will write many kinds of things to evaluate how your training design worked. Opinion questions survey what learners thought and felt as a result of the training. Most of this chapter discussed tests, because test writing differs from other writing, and it is difficult to make tests precise measurements. Checklists, surveys, and tables were reviewed as writing tools that discover and report changes in job performance and contributions to the bottom line. In turn, what deficiencies the measurements and evaluations uncover may lead to new or revised training writing.

To evaluate training, the designer needs to write opinion surveys, tests, job-performance measures, and reports of bottom-line information.

REFERENCES

Dixon, N.M. (1990). *Evaluation: A tool for improving HRD quality.* San Diego, CA: University Associates.

Mager, R.F. (1973). *Measuring instructional intent.* Belmont, CA: Fearon Publishers.

Robinson, D.G., & Robinson, J.C. (1989). *Training for impact: How to link training to business needs and measure the results.* San Francisco: Jossey-Bass.

9

SUPERVISING WRITERS OF TRAINING MATERIALS

Carroll had created a very successful series of self-esteem seminars and ran his own company. Demand for additional training and new seminars including physical activities and nutrition led him to expand and hire designers. Up to this time, he had written all the programs and trained the trainers.

"I want some kind of physical training that would be aerobic, that would be fun, and that also would have an element of teamwork and challenge," he told Samantha, a new designer, and gave her copies of the leaders' guides and materials from his other programs. "Make it like these, with the addition of something physical, you know?"

Near Carroll's office was a cliff that overhung a shallow river. Samantha decided to create an activity involving scaling the cliff and then descending and crossing the river. This would be a week-long course that would include daily aerobic classes to build up endurance and seminars about goal setting, strategizing, and team work. They contracted with a nearby gym for training, but Carroll planned to have his own gym later. Samantha's training map is presented in Figure 9-1.

Carroll approved the map but also wrote these comments on it:

- Get doctor's permission from participants.
- Don't let this cost much.

Training Map

Reach Your Own Height

A Course in Self-Esteem

Objective: Participants will feel confident with new physical challenges.

They will:
    identify goals and roles to work together
    develop planning skills
    strategize various options
    apply these to scaling and descending the cliff.

Time: 1 week

Flow:
Day 1: Introduction and overview; warm-up exercises
    Helicopter tour of cliff
Day 2: Team work
    Sports coach as guest speaker
    Study of various teams and how they work
    Division into teams; volley-ball games against one another
Day 3: Planning and goal setting
    1 hour aerobics in a.m.; 1 hour in p.m.
    Writing clusters
    Video of peak performers
    Recording goals for cliff; dividing labor within teams and
      defining roles
Day 4: Strategic planning
    1 1/2 hour aerobics in a.m.; 1 1/2 hours in p.m.
    Case studies of business strategies: Chrysler; Toyota
    Anticipating obstacles: what if's
    Writing strategy; deciding who does what; how goal will
      be evaluated
Day 5: Carrying out the Plan
    Scaling and descending the cliff
    Discussion of videotapes of the experience
    Celebration

Figure 9-1. Samantha's Training Map

Samantha took out the helicopter ride and replaced some of the expensive speakers with local coaches. Then she wrote the training materials. Carroll handed back her materials covered with red marks, like a school teacher who had let lose on a bad essay. Samantha felt very demoralized from all these negative remarks. She could not understand why Carroll had not explained in greater detail what he wanted. After all, he approved her map. She did not know whether to spend her energies and time now trying to persuade Carroll.

Writing what you as a supervisor want is more efficient than asking the employees to rewrite until they guess what is on your mind. Your writing can help employees feel better about themselves—not only when you write your expectations, but also when you write what the employees do well.

Writing is an extension of a person, even if it is a seemingly impersonal work document. To supervise training writing, the supervisor should be very sensitive about the writer's self embodied on the paper. The supervisor's standards and expectations about the writing should be recorded. When a supervisor receives drafts, he or she should write comments—both positive and negative—right on the pages. A system should be developed for reading subsequent drafts without having to re-read whole documents several times.

WRITE EXPECTATIONS

It is only fair that the supervisor state his or her standards of writing and what is expected instead of saying, "Go do it," then later, "Oh no, that was wrong. It's not what I wanted." As a supervisor, you monitor the requests for training and delegate them to others, so it is your job to set guidelines for how another person could do it. Putting the guidelines in writing increases the communication between you and the person you delegate to and also makes them more permanent. Writing guidelines does not mean you have to create a long procedures manual, although the more particular you are, the longer your guidelines. Neither does recording your expectations stifle another's creativity. You are merely setting limits to fit the qualifications and quality that you need. This whole book has suggested writing standards. You need not write a book. One or two pages is the minimum, and you can write lists or outlines if everyone understands. Figure 9-2 illustrates a supervisor's guidelines.

You owe it to your employees to set limits on their writing, limits based on your ideas of quality and necessary results. Write anything from a one-page list to a several-page document that best communicates with and guides employees to write training materials that work. These standards form the basis of how you evaluate their writing and what you record on their materials.

Design handouts at the same time you write explanations and discussions.

Intros must state:
    attention grabber
    objective
    agenda
    expectations of learning activities

Figure 9-2. Sample Guidelines for Writing Training Materials

WRITE COMMENTS

You will easily discover mistakes and omissions in what other people write. You will help them by writing comments about their writing such as grammar, training issues, and flow. If a writer is not accustomed to your corrections, write out your comments in full, and write more positive comments than negative ones. Blanchard and Johnson (1983) say, "Catch them doing something right," and this applies to managing writing. Let the writers know you have noticed that they no longer make the same mistakes. Find joy in a good writing passage. Write "good" if nothing else; but if you can, be specific. For example, you might write, "good transition," "great symbol," or "wonderful, creative application." Use other comments that encourage employees to learn and change rather than to feel demoralized. Employees expect comments on their work. Otherwise, there would be no reason for you to review it.

CHAPTER SUMMARY

You are almost certain to get several drafts of writing that you delegate. Rather than reading the whole work again each time, you can be more efficient if you devise a system. For example, mark the pages to be changed with post-it notes. Then when the writer has made the changes, look at the change in comparison with the old. You should only have to read the first and last drafts all the way through to see the flow, connections, and completeness.

As a supervisor of writing, you will write less, because someone else does the writing for you. Help those others by recording standards or expectations, by writing positive statements, and by encouraging people to change.

The real measure of writing training materials is the success of the training and use back on the job. As a training writer and supervisor of writers, your reward is in seeing your words come to life and in changing people's work for the better.

REFERENCE

Blanchard, K. & Johnson, S. (1983). *The one minute manager.* New York: Berkley Books.

BIBLIOGRAPHY

Blanchard, K. & Johnson, S. (1983). *The one minute manager.* New York: Berkley Books.

Byham, W.C. with Cox, J. (1988). *Zapp! The lightning of empowerment.* Pittsburgh, PA: Development Dimensions International Press. (Available from University Associates, San Diego, CA.)

Davies, I.K. (1981). *Instructional technique.* New York: McGraw-Hill.

Field, S. (1984). *Screen writers' workbook.* New York: Dell.

Forbess-Greene, S. (1983). *The encyclopedia of icebreakers.* San Diego, CA: University Associates.

Laird, D. (1978). *Approaches to training and development.* Reading, MA: Addison-Wesley.

Laubach, F.C., Kirk, E.M., & Laubach, R.S. (1983). *The Laubach way to reading (Skill Book 3).* Syracuse, NY: New Readers Press.

McLagan, P.A. (1978). *Helping others learn: Designing programs for adults.* Reading, MA: Addison-Wesley.

Mager, R.F. (1962). *Preparing instructional objectives.* Palo Alto, CA: Fearon Publishers.

Mager, R.F. (1973). *Measuring instructional intent.* Belmont, CA: Fearon Publishers.

Matrazzo, D. (1985). *The corporate scriptwriting book.* Portland, OR: Communicom Publishing.

Mitchell, G. (1987). *The trainer's handbook.* New York: Amacom.

Newstrom, J.W. & Scannell, E.E. (1980). *Games trainers play.* New York: McGraw-Hill.

Pfeiffer, J.W., & Jones, J.E. (Eds.). (1969, 1970, 1971, 1973, 1975, 1977, 1979, 1981, 1983, 1985). *A handbook of structured experiences for human relations training* (Vols. I-X). San Diego, CA: University Associates.

Pfeiffer, J.W., & Ballew, A.C. (1988). *Design skills in human resource development.* San Diego, CA: University Associates.

Robinson, D.G., & Robinson, J.C. (1989). *Training for impact: How to link training to business needs and measure the results.* San Francisco: Jossey-Bass.

Wesmen, A.G. Writing the test item. (1979). In R. Thorndike (Ed.), *Educational Measurement.* Washington, D.C.: American Council on Education.

Index

Colophon Page

Editor: Jennifer O. Bryant

Production Editor: Mary Kitzmiller

Cover and Design: Susan G. Odelson

This book was edited and formatted using 386 PC platforms with 8MB RAM and high-resolution, dual-page monitors. The copy was produced using WordPerfect software; pages composed with Ventura software; illustrations produced in Corel Draw or hand-drawn. The text is set in Stone Serif 11/13 points and heads in Optima. Proof copies were printed on a 400-dpi laser printer and final camera-ready output on a 1200-dpi laser imagesetter by Pfeiffer & Company.